THE MARIE STORY

THE MARIE STORY

Peter Rowland

Copyright © Peter Rowland 2005

First Published in 2005 by
Serendipity
Suite 530
37 Store Street
Bloomsbury
London

37 / 39 Victoria Road
Darlington
DL1 5SF

All rights reserved
Unauthorised duplication
contravenes existing laws
British Library Cataloguing-in-Publication data
A catalogue record for this book is available from the British Library
ISBN 1-84394-152-X

Printed and bound by Antony Rowe

For Stanislav and Tereza and, of course, Marie.

Contents

	Acknowledgements	ix
	Preface	xi
I	Marie	1
II	Tereza	17
III	Stanislav	30
IV	Tereza and Stanislav	33
V	Tereza and Marie	36
VI	Marie and Family	52
VII	Marie and Julian	67
VIII	Tereza.	78
IX	Marie – The Last Word.	81

Acknowledgements

The author would like to thank:

H.E. the Ambassador and staff of the Embassy for the Czech Republic in London, for encouragement and smoothing paths in Prague.

Macmillan Publishers Ltd., for kind permission to quote the words of Vaclav Havel in John Simpson's Book 'Strange Places, Questionable People'. 1998

Jiri Rajlich, curator of the Czech Air Force Museum, Kbley.

Iva Spalkova, for friendship and sharing childhood memories.

Dr. Ann Schlee, for valued advice on the format and order of the MS.

John Richardson, for reading the MS and his subsequent trenchant comments.

Cover by Marie: Prague, Charles Bridge and River Vltava

Preface

This is a work of faction, set partly in this country and partly in Czechoslovakia, mainly in the capital city of Prague. It has been written because it is a story of courage and determination that needs to be told and made public. This country turned its back on the Czech's cry for help in the late Nineteen-Thirties and abandoned them to their fate at the hands of the Nazis. Yet many of their nationals escaped and fought with the allies throughout World War Two, and forged friendships that have lasted over the Communist occupation of their country.

Facts. The events in this story happened, just as the main characters lived and – with two exceptions – are still living. To some of the incidents, the author himself was a witness or a participant; others were related to him by one or other of the characters, while some events are history documented and set down.

Fiction. To mould the events of some fifty years into a continuous and readable story, it has been necessary to insert plausible links including the invention of some minor characters; these are of the author's imagination fed by interviews with Czechoslovak nationals both in this country and in Prague. Direct speech conveys the sense of conversations without pretence that they are genuine, wheras the extracts from letters and the quotation from Vaclav Havel are original and accurate.

Stanislav in uniform of an Officer of Czechoslovak Air Force, about 1946.

I

Marie

May 1946

"OK Not bad. Take the blindfold off – have a look round, then we'll do it all again."

In a hangar on an R.A.F. Station in north eastern England, two airmen sat in the cockpit of an aircraft.

"Off – take it off! – like switches … ON … OFF!"

The man in the left-hand seat pulled off the scarf and grinned sheepishly: a big fellow, solid, substantial – in contrast to his younger, much slimmer instructor sitting alongside him in the navigator's seat.

"Look round: take it in logical sections – look at your notes – think in English, not Czech."

Stanislav Židlický, born in Domažlice about a hundred miles south west of the capital, joined the Czechoslovak Air Force in 1936 and qualified originally as a Navigator before the German Army marched into Prague in 1939.

One of the first actions of the occupying power was to disarm all Czechoslovak military units, and then commence a policy of dispersing personnel into civilian occupations. Gradually, in two's and three's, officers and enlisted men alike found themselves as clerks or warehousemen often in a part of the country with which they were unfamiliar.

"OK Blindfold – scarf – ON again."

Stanislav was allocated to work in a large office block belonging to the City authorities in the centre of Prague. There he endured the privations and humiliations – and dangers – forced upon the population of an occupied city.

"Right. Hand on compass … yes, that's it. Oxygen valve – OK. Now giro adjust … no, no, no! Blindfold off and find it!"

With the end of the war came the re-formation of the Czechoslovak Air Force. But the Germans had destroyed or commandeered their aircraft and equipment, so some fifty Czechoslovak aircrew including a number who had escaped and fought with the Allies found themselves in England learning to fly a British aircraft. They had to be tested and passed before collecting new aircraft from the factory and flying them out to Prague to form the first post-war Czechoslovak Squadron. The first step in that process was to memorise every dial, switch and lever in an unfamiliar cockpit. Aircrew of the 1940's had to be able to operate any control without looking down.

"OK, now we'll have a stab at the figures."

"Stabbat?"

"Oh, sorry. No – forget it – look in your Notes. Engine temperatures and pressures – turn over – next page. There ... think you know them?"

Another half hour, then, "Right, that's enough. Time for a beer before lunch." They walked across the tarmac towards the Mess. Now they were relaxed, companionable – the earnest endeavours of student and instructor behind them. Indeed there was a neat reversal of standing for the 'student' was by far the more experienced airman and of a higher rank than his young instructor.

Charles pushed his way through the crowd round the small bar. "Two pints, please, George," and signed his Bar book, soggy from over-spill on the formica top.

"Cheers!"

"Na zdraví! Where we go tonight, Sharles?"

"We'll try that place down by the river – the Chequers. Have we taken you there?"

"No."

"OK. Let's get Derek and his man along – make up a party. Won't be long now. If the weather holds, we'll have you all airborne by the end of the week. How's the technical side going?"

And they wandered off for lunch, mingling with the others. The dining-room waiter by the door heard snatches of conversation: "How did your chap get on with Heike last weekend? ...

"Snowing in Prague yet? They're devils to land if the runway's wet ..."

"Seen the Flight Commander's new red-head? ..."

The waiter listened but he'd heard it all before.

In the evenings they relaxed. Out of uniform, no formalities, the beer flowed, the laughter erupted. Despite the language difficulties, the camaraderie engendered by the dangers and privations of war prevailed. An unlikely bond had grown between Stanislav and Charles; their morning handshakes firm and confident, their evening salutations cheerful and trusting. Charles knew that his man was intelligent – his work in the cockpit showed that – but there was so much more he wanted to know. Where had he spent the war years? What gave him his quiet confidence? The solid reliability and coolness of the man suggested so many possibilities. He watched Stanislav down a pint of best British bitter, his eyes darting from speaker to speaker. Laughter was never far away yet something in those eyes convinced him that Stanislav had known danger, and hardship, and maybe treachery. Was it simply the language or an unassuming modesty that prevented him from talking? All he's told me about himself, thought Charles, is that he's not married, and I can tell for myself that he knows his way around an aircraft. That's it!

Charles looked round at the faces of Stanislav and his Czech colleagues who had each been through their own particular hells; there was no despair, no resignation ... only the dream of the new heaven each hoped to create in the homeland they had not seen for years.

Back off Christmas Leave 1946, Charles was at a loose end pending another posting. The job with the Czechoslovaks had been a one-off; not helpful career-wise, but on the whole he had enjoyed it. For a fleeting moment he even considered putting in for a full Instructor's Course, but then thought better of it. Instead, he wrote a postcard to Captain S. Židlický, Czechoslovak Air Force, Prague. The picture showed a pub in Wharfedale where they had drunk together.

In fact, it was a rather special pub – the scene of Stanislav's linguistic triumph, for he had taken the order for his six companions to the bar; returned with the right drinks, the right change, and accepted their congratulations with, "Bloody good, ya?"

Six months later, Charles was flying a desk at a Headquarters unit. Despite this being peacetime and their role far from secret, Security demanded the unit being accommodated in a large rambling house on the outskirts of a small market town.

On a bright June morning, the mail landed on Charles' desk. From it spilled a postcard with a picture of a beautiful bridge over a wide river: the legend read, "Charles Bridge, Praha." Charles chuckled with delight and turned it over. There he read, "Dear Friend, You are well? I fly your lovely British aircraft but not in snow. It is hot here now. Na zdraví! Stanislav."

Charles pinned it to the noticeboard over his desk: he had accumulated half a dozen more before finally taking them down, and moving on.

In 1950, Charles – now a civilian – married the girl of his dreams. Shortly afterwards, a letter arrived with Czechoslovakian stamps and Prague postmark.

"It's from your Czech friend," said his wife, Mary, passing it over the breakfast table.

"No, not his handwriting," Charles replied, staring at the envelope. "Besides it's over a year now since his last postcard."

"Well, why not open it and see?"

Charles slit open the envelope. "Good Lord, it's from his wife! but hang on – Stanislav's not married."

"Well, he is now!" retorted Mary.

Charles read in silence, then very quietly, "No, he's not – he's dead."

He finished reading and then turning back to the beginning, read aloud.

"*Surely you don't know who is writing to you – I am wife of your friend Stanislav Židlický to whom you were writing last Christmas. Stanislav has married me on 21st December 1948. Now I must to tell you that your friend is on 4th*

March 1949 dead – you will surely know how it happened in flying accident ...'
Then she goes on to say that she has found our correspondence in Stanislav's papers, and would like to continue writing to his friend in England ... oh, but we're not to ask questions; that makes things difficult. Her name's Tereza, by the way. Finally, she says that a daughter, Marie, was born in September last year ..."

Charles passed the letter over to Mary. "I'll bet she learnt her English in school. Doesn't sound right – it's as if she's read it but never heard it spoken."

"What a peculiar thing to say! Out of the blue comes a remarkable letter with news of the death of an old friend, and a birth, and all you can do is to criticise the writer's English!"

"Now I didn't mean to ..."

"You couldn't do anything like as well in Czech, could you? Could you?"

The rebuke hung in the air.

Charles pushed his chair back, stood and poured himself an other mug of coffee. He paced slowly round the small kitchen, aware that Mary's eyes followed him. She had laid the letter beside her plate; Charles paused and re-read over her shoulder the second paragraph.

"I don't like that '... flying accident ...' Stanislav could be a bit wild in the pub of an evening, but he was a first-rate airman. Checked everything. If it was an accident it would be something sudden like a mid-air collision."

"You said, 'If it was an accident' ..."

"It's just that guys with Stanislav's temperament rarely have accidents. And I don't trust whoever is pulling the strings in Prague; they're out of the same stable as the guys who closed the frontiers into Berlin and caused such chaos a year ago. Any device to make life difficult for the West ... and Stanislav had come back out of the West."

Mary sighed. "OK," apologised Charles, "current affairs lecture over. But I'd love to know if any of the other guys in that squadron have had accidents."

"Well, you're not to ask questions, remember? And if you're going to work today, you'd better look sharp ... so had I!"

The remains of breakfast were abandoned. Over her shoulder Mary shouted, "Tell me tonight if you're going to write back."

Charles' head re-appeared momentarily round the door, "Tell you now," he said, "I'm writing this evening!" and the door slammed.

He did indeed write that evening, and thus began a correspondence which was to last many years. Tereza wrote regularly at Christmas, Easter, and from an uncle's retreat in the mountains during the summer. Her letters were confined to family news; to brief descriptions of her city, and the highlands to the north east near the Polish Border. Each letter told, with mother's pride barely concealed, of the growth and development of her daughter, Marie, and a copy of the annual photograph added to a growing collection; each ended with an invitation to visit Prague.

Tabor. 29th of August, 1951.
I wish to you and your wife that you soon have a baby as I have. It is really a pleasure. Many thanks for your letter and photographs, I thought you are no more living when I did not so long hear from you. I send you photograph of my daughter, Marie, here she is one year ten months old ... If you come to Prague you will be my guest ...

Prague 18th of December 1952. I have very long not hear from you. I do not know if you have move. I await answer and then shall send you new photograph of Marie who was 3 years old in September. Have you not also a baby? We have snow and it is very cold now. For Christmas I send best wishes and for New Year ...

About herself and her late husband – never a word.

Only once did Tereza attempt something more. In 1953, Charles and Mary received their usual Easter letter, but it was the envelope which interested them.

"I've not seen one like this since before the war." Charles fingered the delicate blue, tissue-paper lining.

"They were considered rather posh, even in those days," responded Mary.

On an impulse, Charles tore the lining out of the envelope: stuck between them were six Czech stamps of a high denomination, each bearing the head of Jan Masaryk.

For a moment, neither moved.

"Well, that little lot must have cost her all of £5 – and I'll bet she could ill-afford it."

"It's a message," said Mary. "Remember what happened to Masaryk four years ago – it's the only way Tereza could think of to convey what she obviously can't write. Don't ask questions, she said." She paused, then thoughtfully, "I wonder if anyone reads our letters before they reach her ..."

Charles wrote that thought in large letters on the cover of the airmail writing pad.

The years passed by, and in the Sixties a new Communist leader, Alexander Dubček, came to power in Czechoslovakia. Very gradually, a new spirit of liberalism was detected. Press censorship was relaxed and by degrees the import of foreign literature was introduced. Not that it made much impact on Charles' household; there were major milestones – a son, Daniel, and then later a daughter, Emma, arrived bringing joy, laughter and total chaos. Professional advancement meant moving house – three times – with all the disruption that that adventure entails. The last move promised a period of stability, and with the children settled into school Charles and Mary could breathe again.

MARIE

Marie 'sixteen going on seventeen'.

It became evident that Tereza was teaching her daughter English. Holiday postcards, in careful juvenile writing, started to arrive.

25 July 1960. Dear Charles and Mary, I send you many regards from Sněžka. Your Marie. On the reverse, a delightful mountain scene.

Tereza's letters continued the regular pattern throughout the Sixties. One morning when the later than usual Easter letter had arrived from Prague, Danny lounged over the breakfast table gazing at the new photograph of Marie – 16 going on 17 – long, dark hair, deep blue eyes and with a touch of the glamour that only some studio portraits can give.

"Dad," Danny ventured cautiously, "can we invite her over for the summer hols?"

Emma immediately latched on. "Great! She'll be on my side, won't she Mum? Oh, go on, Dad, can we?"

Emma was at the stage when she hated all boys – largely because her particular friends said they hated all boys, and though Daniel was the exception she included him as a matter of face. In Marie, she saw an ally through the long, hot days of summer. Daniel's motive was not quite so clear.

Charles and Mary discussed the suggestion in bed that night. "It's a tremendous responsibility we'd be taking on." Mary, practical as ever went on, "You know what our two can be like; well, just add one high-spirited 16 year-old girl, whom we've never seen ... "

"How do you know she's high-spirited?"

"You saw her photograph!"

"Yes, and so did Daniel, ... I reckon he's interested ... "

"That just makes it worse ... and I'll bet she can't speak a word of English. No, I'm against it; the risks are too great."

"Ah, don't you remember ... that letter ... Easter last year was it? ... when Tereza said she was teaching Marie to read English ... and those postcards?"

"Mmmm ... but she won't be anything like fluent."

They both lay thinking.

"Well, I'd like to think I did something for poor old Stanislav. Mind you, I doubt very much whether they'd allow her to come, despite the relaxations there."

"They might say she could come only with her Mother, then not allow either back in again – then we really would have a problem on our hands."

"No, they wouldn't do that; that's not the way they think. They've spent time and money on the girl and they'll want some return for it: she's young and useful. Remember Tereza's last letter – the one where she says that Marie has been selected to go to that Art College in Prague? Even allowing for parental pride, it indicates Marie has talent. No, Tereza stays there – that way they know the girl will return."

"Yes," said Mary slowly, "that does make sense. OK, let's invite her – just for the holiday, but I'll be as surprised as you if she makes it. We'll tell our two in the morning."

And so Miss M. Židlická was invited to spend August as the guests of friends in England.

Tereza's reply was by return. She was delighted that Marie could come to England to see the country where her late husband had made so many friends, and would apply to the authorities for permission. Their reply was not by return, but to everyone's astonishment, permission (with conditions) was eventually granted for her to spend one month in England the following year. Daniel and Emma were delighted and told all their friends, while Charles and Mary – hiding a degree of apprehension – told their friends about an old wartime alliance bearing fruit.

"Wait till they see her," said Charles, "the camera cannot lie!"

"Yes, well, she'll be here while we're on holiday. You did realise that?" Mary pointed out.

"Of course, she'll liven it up, I'll bet."

"Right, you'd better get on the phone to Ken and ask if that cottage they've taken in Cornwall can sleep nine. We're five now, remember."

They met her off the plane at Heathrow one bright morning in late July 1966. 'Wearing a red coat,' the letter had said, and they did not have long to wait; a long, bright red coat emerged from Customs, and then they were waving and shouting and ... and Marie waved and shouted, and hugged them all, and then hugged them all again ... and burst into tears ...

Even Charles had a lump in his throat. 'Yes,' he thought, 'you're Stanislav's daughter all right. The eyes, the set of the face ... I knew him only for a few weeks all those years ago, and now he's back ... and she's every bit as striking as that photograph – given that's she's just completed her first unaccompanied flight into the maelstrom of a foreign airport ... and she's crying ...'

"Come on, troops," he said, "we're causing an obstruction. Let's move."

Indeed later travellers were having to manoeuvre round either side of the animated group, and so Marie with one arm linked through Mary's and the other through Emma's with Daniel carrying her case, walked, climbed and descended through the maze that is Heathrow to the car park.

Charles unlocked the car. Marie stared. "For us?" she asked.

"Yes, this is ours." Daniel explained.

They had placed Marie between Daniel and Emma on the back seat, and as they wound their way down five floors of the car park, Mary heard her ask again about the car.

Her command of the English language was minimal, but she was able to make herself understood with the help of a small book which she frequently drew from the deep pocket of her coat. The Czech – English dictionary was well-thumbed in those first few days, and often it was passed to Daniel when the pronunciation of a word was in doubt.

"Yes," Daniel repeated, "this is our car. Not a (dictionary) taxi, nor a bus (there are buses in Prague) but ours. Does your Mother have a car?"

"No, we cannot have one."

Neither Emma nor Daniel understood this. Mary turned round and joined in. By many questions and much use of the dictionary it became clear that in her country it was difficult to own a car. If you were a member of the Communist Party you had a chance to own one – but only after a long wait in the pecking order. It was true that some people had a car only because they had managed to keep one which they owned before 1939. More often than not you queued at the stop like everybody else. Buses and trams were part of the socialist way of living in the City; Marie thought nothing of it because she had grown up with it.

Daniel shook his head in amazement. 'This,' thought Mary to herself, 'is going to be quite a month..'

Charles chose the longer, scenic route home. At one point, they came into to a small seaside town, down to the front and then along the coast for a short distance. Suddenly, Marie asked, "What is that?"

Silence in the back. They looked; there was nothing obvious; typical sort of front; beach, groups on the sand, some bathers.

"What is that? There, there ... " and she pointed across Daniel with a sweep of her hand.

'Oh, my God,' guessed Charles, 'of course! Czechoslovakia's landlocked. She's never seen the sea before!'

He stopped the car. Emma opened her door and Marie was out, across the road and running down the beach, Emma flying after her.

Mary and Charles looked at each other. "What have we taken on?" sighed Mary.

"You know, they advertise these expensive Adventure Holidays. We've got this one for free. Come on ... you're the one with Life Saving experience."

Marie had stopped at the sea's edge, staring, uncomprehending. A few moments later, she kicked off her shoes and took the first tentative steps into the water. A yelp, a laugh; ... it was colder than she had expected ... then back in again. A few steps further, then she turned – and laughing – danced in circles as the waves played around her ankles. Emma and Daniel lost no time joining in, and the little group raced along the sand until panting with exertion and delight, they threw themselves down at Mary's feet. The bottom of Marie's coat was a darker red, and Mary wondered whether the girl would return to Prague with her coat several inches shorter than when she came.

Eventually, they trailed back up to the road and the car. Marie turned, shook her long, dark hair and looked again at the sweep of the sea; wordless.

'Well,' thought Charles as he drove the short distance home, 'that's three firsts. Her first flight ; her first sight of the sea, and a drive in a car that goes where it wants – not where it's sent. Not a bad start!'

But there was another delight in store before Marie finally fell asleep. Charles and Mary lived on the edge of a small town in a large and rambling house, the core of which was Tudor. Emma took Marie up to her bedroom.

It was the normal guest room; double bed, chest of drawers, built-in wardrobe, chairs, flowers on the dresser. The window looked out onto the road.

Then Emma showed her the bathroom next door. "You and Danny and I share that," she explained. "Mum and Dad have their own at the back of the house."

Marie turned back into her room. She searched briefly and then asked Emma where her things were. So Emma took her to her room, then flung open the door to Danny's room and shut it quickly. "It's always such a mess, but that's boys for you!"

Marie looked completely puzzled.

"You have each rooms?"

"Yes, of course. We used to creep in with Mum and Dad when we were little, but that was years ago! Why? What's the matter?"

Over supper, with the dictionary in constant use and despite Marie's original ideas of English syntax, it became clear that to have her own bedroom was another first.

She and her mother lived in a fourth-floor flat, the lift to which rarely worked ("So my big legs by ... mmm ... stairs," an explanation which had everyone laughing.) The flat had a largish sitting room which converted into a bedroom at night which she and her mother shared; a breakfast / living room and a kitchen with a bathroom off. Marie gave the idea that while it was rather old-fashioned, it was larger than they might expect for a mother and daughter family.

Daniel went to bed very thoughtful; Marie was lying in her own bed gazing at the ceiling when Mary looked in. "You are all so kind," she said simply.

Marie

One thing the children had in common was their schools, and an early visit was to the school at which Daniel was a student, and to which Emma would be going in the September Term. It was at the evening meal that the questions were debated, and the differences sorted out.

Marie could not make out what all the fields were for. "Play games?" she asked incredulously. "In Prague, we do not ... mmm ... play for time!"

Daniel, assuming the role of Teacher of English for a Foreign Student, firmly corrected her. "You mean time for playing, not playing for time – which means something quite different."

He was shouted down by three female voices at once, but through the hubbub put up a stout defence. "You won't let me get away with faulty grammar in French homework, so we ought to tell Marie when she makes mistakes. That's only right, isn't it? You want to speak English correctly, don't you, Marie?"

A smile crossed Marie's face. "Danny, do you speak Russian?"

Emma chimed in, "Oh, yes, Mummy, at Marie's school they all have to learn Russian. And ... and ... I think Marie said she could speak German as well. Is that right?"

"Yes, I have Russian since nine, and then later German, so I speak easy ... "

Charles looked straight at Danny just in case – but Danny had become engrossed in his supper. Mary also found her plate of interest – pondering on the thought that the girl on the other side of the table could at the least make herself understood in three languages beside her native tongue. 'And what have we got?' she thought, 'school French, most of which I've forgotten!'

"And there was something else," said Emma, "which I couldn't understand."

Out came the Dictionary. From the huddle at one end of the table came Mary's explanation. "She wanted to know where the Training part of the school was. Apparently, all Czech pupils have to undertake some form of vocational training as well as academic studies. What are you being trained for, Marie?"

"... mmm ... for printing ... in books, papers. At school ... and in College."

Daniel looked up. "Do you mean you can print now?"

"Yes, ... mmm ... machines I use."

Charles chipped in. "Would you like to go round our local printing works? Yes? I think I can arrange that. I'll phone Stephen in the morning."

But the following morning had been reserved for the girls. Marie was amazed that all pupils wore similar clothing for school – a uniform in fact – and so Mary said that they would go to the appointed shop and buy Emma's new uniform. On the way, Mary did her best to disabuse Marie of any militaristic thinking behind this custom; it was, she tried to explain, a way of ensuring that parental wealth – or lack of it – was not apparent to other pupils. "That would not occur in our country," Marie countered; Mary smiled indulgently, "We'll sort that out over supper. Here we are" and she lead the way into the clothing shop.

"Right," said the assistant, "we'll have to measure you, young lady."

Emma looked up enquiringly at Mary, and Marie – who had a figure well worth measuring – indicated with her finger a circle round her chest, her waist and her hips – and then winked. Emma was delighted: for the first time she was being treated as really feminine. She held her arms out sideways and waited breathlessly for the results. Poor Emma! No matter how many times or with what ingenuity the assistant tried, he could not but make an inch or two difference in all three measurements.

"I'm just straight up and down!" howled Emma.

Marie laughed until tears ran down her cheeks; Mary's shoulders shook until she had to turn away. At last, Marie folded Emma in her arms and assured her that one day she would have a figure like hers, ... but what finally consoled her was when both promised they would not say a word to Daniel or Charles.

And nothing about Emma's shape was said at supper, but it was Marie who asked what Mary had meant about differences in parental wealth. Daniel explained that different jobs were paid at different rates, usually according to difficulty – and in any case, some people were not employed by others but worked for themselves.

Marie said that in her country all people were paid according to their job but on a much lower scale. If you were someone important, say in the Government, you had a better flat so you could entertain foreign dignitaries: if you were a vet, you had a vehicle to get around farms. She said that was a very fair system.

"Hogwash!" said Daniel.

"What is 'Hogvash'?"

"It's a veterinary expression," interjected Charles hurriedly. "Have another dumpling?"

Next morning, they all had dental appointments so Charles invited Marie to go with him on a visit to a neighbouring town. He began by calling for petrol at his local garage where he had an account. Marie watched with interest while he operated the pump and followed him to the door of the office where he signed a chit for the petrol.

"Oo's the stunner then?" murmured the lad behind the desk.

"Never you mind!" retorted Charles, and ushering Marie back into the car, they went on their way.

Later that evening, Emma sidled up to Mary preparing the meal and asked, "Mummy, is Daddy very important?"

"Why on earth do you ask that?"

"Well, Marie said he must be a very important person because he didn't pay for his petrol this morning. She says she's writing to her mother tonight telling her all about us and England."

Marie

What Marie wrote to her mother they never found out, though she did admit to having said that while she could usually understand what the family said to her, they had difficulty understanding what she said to them! She did tell her mother about the man on the plane though.

Sitting next to her was a middle-aged Englishman who had been to Prague on business. They struck up a conversation, and he praised her courage for venturing alone into a Western country. He asked whether she was worried about anything, and she admitted to an apprehension over money. One of the conditions laid down by the Czech authorities was that she could take little money out of the country – they permitted her to take two hundred and fifty Czech Crowns, worth about £5 sterling. Before the end of the holiday, she might have to ask for pocket money ...

Her travelling companion thought for a few moments, and then talked to the people on the other side of the aisle; then to the passengers in the row behind; the row in front. Shortly before they landed, he gave Marie a handful of coins. "That," he said, "is for you to buy a gift for your mother, and something for your hosts." And people round about shook her hand or patted her arm or just smiled as they left the aircraft. "Enjoy your stay!" they had said.

She was certainly doing that!

Marie gained in confidence daily. Charles arrived home one evening and Mary took him on one side before the evening meal.

"Would you like the story of the day?"

"Yes. You're going to tell me anyway."

"We lost her this morning – couldn't find her anywhere. So we left the back door open, a note on the table, and went in search."

"From the noise in the next room I take it you found her. So where?"

"In the market. You know that stall just past the post office corner – the one that sells red underwear and ... "

"Oh, no ... "

"Nylon knickers ... She'd bought dozens! All sizes and colours! I asked her what on earth she wanted so many for and she said they would be ideal presents for all her friends. You can't get them for love or money in Czechoslovakia because the factory near Prague had burnt down and not been rebuilt. So I persuaded her to cut down a bit or she'd need an export licence!"

"Not a bad idea though – simple and not taking much space in her luggage. I presume you gave her a good ticking off for disappearing like that."

Indeed Mary had, but there were times when Marie just could not resist temptation.

Their holiday that year was combined with old friends who had two daughters of ages not dissimilar to Daniel and Emma. The cottage in Cornwall was ideal and flexible enough to accommodate the newly-enlarged party. Ken and Mavis' two were delighted to have an older and very glamorous girl in their midst, especially as she was so jolly and said such funny things but at supper on the second night, Marie was nowhere to be found.

Mary was worried. "She's not in the cottage or the garden. None of us know the area, nor does she – and it's dusk. Where on earth has she got to?"

"I think I can guess," said Charles. "You have your suppers and if I'm not back when you've finished, you can all come and find me!"

Charles walked down to the shore, and saw Marie some distance away sitting on a rock gazing out to sea. Charles approached quietly and sat down beside her.

"Charles, was my father brave man?"

"Yes, my dear, very brave."

She sat with her knees drawn up, her arms clasped round her legs, staring at the ripples in the quiet sea.

"Why did he have to die like that – before I could know him?"

"One day, I promise, you will find out much more about him and what really happened."

They sat silently for several minutes more. Then as if satisfied, Marie stood up. "Is Mary angry?"

"Very!"

Arm-in-arm, they trudged up the shore, then up the lane to the cottage. "Come on, you two," encouraged Ken, "supper's nearly all gone!"

Marie made her peace with Mary that night.

If at times she caused anxiety, she also provided much fun and amusement. Fascinated by the difference in payment for different jobs, Marie, quite early in the holiday, produced her little notebook and sitting down by Ken asked what he did for a living. Taken aback, Ken said that he was a Lecturer at a College where Teachers were trained.

Notebook out and pencil poised, Marie then asked, "What money do you get for this?"

She could not understand his embarrassment. Charles tried to explain, "You see, Marie, this is something we just don't talk about. Ken's salary is private to him; Mavis's is private to her."

Marie turned, "What do you work at, Mavis?"

"I'm what's called a Social Worker. I look after poor people, unfortunate people . . .

A different tack. "Do you get more money than Ken?"

"Off to the beach with you!" Mary sprang to the rescue and shooed all the children out.

As they walked down, Charles apologised and tried to explain. "You see, things are different in her country and what Marie's trying to do is make comparisons between their living conditions and ours. One day she had our rather formidable Postmaster backed up into a corner, asking him all sorts of questions about his wages. I think Mary reached the Post Office in the nick of time."

Thereafter Ken and Mavis talked much with Marie about life in Czechoslovakia, and the holiday sped by. Then came the re-packing ('Who's got my towel? Where's my other sandal?'), and it was back to work; to school, and for Marie – back to Heathrow. There were Goodbyes, and Remembers, and Hugs and Don't forgets, and Goodbyes again, and Waves and Write soon ... and then Marie was gone ... back to her mother, Teresa, and the flat in Bubeneč, and to start work at the Grafická Škola, that prestigious Printing College in Prague.

While life returned to some degree of normality and routine in Charles' and Mary's household, they all agreed it would never be quite the same again. They had had not just a friend over for the holiday: it had been much more than that. It had been an experience which none would forget, they had all – in different ways – been touched by this girl who had come into their lives and opened windows for them. Mary summed it up neatly – and prophetically – when she said, "I rather hope we haven't seen the last of Marie!" with which sentiment the whole family agreed.

They had certainly not heard the last of Marie. Letters flew back and forth. Marie wrote of her work and of her holidays spent largely, and compulsorily, in the service of the Communist system. She and her friends worked in the public parks collecting chestnuts and acorns. They went round the streets collecting newspapers and magazines for re-cycling; there was competition between groups to see who could collect the greatest weight. During the following summer holiday Marie was picking hops, an activity which prompted Charles' memory. "Do you remember hearing about the parties of Londoners who went every year down into Kent picking hops? "

"Yes, weren't they from the East End? It was their annual holiday and they got paid for it as well." said Mary. "Like the casual labourers who always arrived at our farm regularly for the harvest. Many were Irish lads who turned up every year. They seemed to enjoy it." Then after a pause, "Are we going to invite Marie for next summer's holiday? She'll have taken her Final Exams by then, and I doubt if she will want to go picking hops again. She'll be ... what ... nearly nineteen by next August."

So the question was put to the family, and by unanimous agreement Marie was invited to spend the summer holiday of 1968 back in England again.

If it had been a sixteen year old girl whom the family had seen off at Heathrow in 1966, it was a young lady whom they welcomed back two years later. The same Marie, with her freshness and fun and vitality, but self-confident, assured and certainly better informed.

It would be just to attribute this to natural development, but there was a further factor.

In the early Sixties, a man named Alexander Dubček had risen to the top of the Communist Party in Czechoslovakia, and to general surprise (and some apprehension in the Warsaw Pact countries) began to modify the standard isolationist policy. Gradually he persuaded his colleagues to permit a limited amount of foreign news to circulate in Czechoslovak newspapers, on radio and television. This – proving popular – was followed by the restricted import of some western literature.

There was no doubt that this change of policy had an effect, and it was the family's turn to be surprised at Marie's knowledge of Western affairs. Limited though this was, it was infinitely more than she had displayed in 1966 and Marie herself acknowledged that 'information' was more readily available: it had been, she said, their 'Springtime of Freedom'.

The end of Marie's holiday was approaching; only a few days remained. She had bought a present for her Mother and small gifts for all her host family – even a tin of very special food for the cat.

Just about in time thought Charles, who had followed mid-European news with some anxiety. The recent spirit of freedom initiated by the Dubček regime was viewed with disapproval by neighbouring Warsaw Pact countries. There had been an anti-Dubček campaign in the Soviet Press; a build-up of troops along the Border, but talks between Soviet and Czech leaders did not deter Dubček from his policies. Charles believed there would be only another few weeks before the storm broke.

It was the 21st August 1968. Before their evening meal, the family had been watching television. Marie liked news broadcasts, still amazed at the criticism of governmental figures permitted in the media. It was six o'clock: as the sounds of Big Ben died away, the screen was filled with the sight of tanks and mobile troops. The voice-over announced, "This morning at dawn, sixty thousand troops from Warsaw Pact Countries invaded Czechoslovakia. There are no reports of casualties, but an official news black-out has been imposed. These pictures from our special correspondent in Prague . . ."

Everyone in the room fell silent, tense, gazing at the screen. Another picture of tanks grinding down a wide street. The camera panned round; no one; nothing; deserted as far as the eye could see, except for the monstrous machines of war.

Another shot; soldiers, expressionless, sitting down each side of open lorries, their rifles between their knees.

Suddenly Marie shouted, "There, that's our street, that's where we live. There, that big block of ..." but the camera had moved on.

Some minutes later the announcer said, "We shall bring you further news from Prague as soon as it comes in. Now for the rest of the day's news ..."

Marie rushed from the room and they heard the front door slam. Emma and Daniel tore after her.

"No!" said Charles very firmly, "No, come back Danny, Emma. This is one occasion when we're not going after her." They returned reluctantly. "No, my dears, this is something that Marie has to face alone. The only thing we can do is to be here when she returns, and give her what comfort and courage we can."

"Yes," said Mary, "Your Dad's quite right. Come and help me make supper." But no one was very hungry.

An hour later, Marie returned. She shut the kitchen door quietly behind her. A deep intake of breath; her hair tossed back and with head held high, she looked at each in turn and finally at Charles.

"I have made up my mind – I am not going back. Can I stay with your family?"

"What about your Mother?"

"We have lived under Soviet Communism for twenty years. She will understand ..."

II

Tereza

1955. PRAGUE

It was icy in the little room. Winter had come early; there had already been snow which had turned first to slush and then to ice as the temperature dropped. The City lay beneath its mantle uncomfortably; each step in the street potential danger as darkness fell over the old town.

Tereza bustled round to keep warm. She, her mother and her six-year old daughter, Marie, lived in a stone-built, former palace, converted into flats by the Communists on Karmelitská Ulice, a street not far from the river and running parallel to it. Behind the flats the great grass slope of the Petřín rose high to the crest where the radio mast stood, dominating the skyline. In the centre of the building was a large archway, large enough to have accommodated a horse and cart in days long gone. This cobbled entrance lead up the slope to a courtyard with access to some of the flats, to outhouses and stores.

Theirs was a ground floor flat towards the back of the building, and therefore more below ground than above. In the little bedroom, the only window ran along the north east wall high above the dresser; in early morning light she could see passing feet and legs descending the slope towards the roadway. It had been a childhood pastime to watch and guess, matching the feet to the unseen owners on their way to work. Some she knew; the tram driver with his big boots was usually the first, then the smart shoes of the hotel receptionist, and the young couple who – though from different apartments – used to meet opposite her window and then disappear in step. And she remembered the time when she first saw the jackboots – black, shiny, hard. She always knew when they were coming; they were heard before they were seen and apprehension rose in her throat. There was never just one pair, always two or more. Tereza fought the memory down; turned and checked that Marie was sound asleep.

Quickly she undressed placing each garment on the chair; drew out the long linen nightie from beneath the pillow and slipped in beside her daughter whose encircling warmth did not extend to the bottom of the bed. Tereza gasped with the shock. She lay tight within herself seeking warmth, and listened.

She could hear her mother in the next room, breathily drifting in and out of sleep. The china stove in the main room hummed gently, maintaining life at the base of the stone building where each of the three floors above seemed to press down as if to extinguish wherever life there was below ground. Outside there was little movement, no footfalls on the icy slope. She heard a solitary vehicle approach and pass – taking longer than normal. The intense cold from the cloudless sky seemed to have frozen the entire city into immobility. Tereza hugged herself more closely, and drifted.

And there it was, that long shiny wooden box, carried high on the shoulders of faceless men in peaked caps and long greatcoats swaying ahead of the procession of chanting men and women. Then it was lowered and the bearers stood to one side while the singing congregation slowly filed towards the box, now suspended in mid-air; weightless in time and space. And she, Tereza, carried along in her mother's arms, gliding towards it until she could see, lying inside, her father.

No, not her father as she had known him but a caricature, a hideous model, a demon. Dressed in a military coat, the body's shrunken neck protruded from the collar while the decayed head looked to have the skin drawn tightly over the skull. Where the eyes had been – those deep, dark brown eyes that had twinkled with merriment – were simply black holes, and the mouth shut tight in grim silence. His black hair had been combed unnaturally forward over his forehead as if to cover as much of his face as possible.

The sequence ended as it always did; the few moments of disbelief brought to an abrupt halt as a dark shiny lid was slammed down; the box lifted again onto the shoulders of the bearers and borne away into darkness.

Tereza woke with her own crying, and Marie stirring. "Hush now, back to sleep, little one," she whispered as the girl sought the comfort of her mother's arms. And in the silence, Tereza tried yet again to erase the memory. Logical adult explanation that her father had contracted typhoid; that he had lain frozen on the battlefield for days; that it was filial duty to view a father in his coffin counted for little. She knew she would wake exhausted; would perform the morning's chores with speedy exasperation, and arrive at the City Council's offices in a bad temper. It would, more than usually, be a day for keeping her mouth shut.

Tereza's journey to work took some twenty minutes. She walked to the junction with Mostecká Street, caught one of the frequent trams into the New Town, and then a few steps brought her to the Council's offices in the Žižkov area of the city. The tram ride was relaxation, yet on this morning another memory stirred and rose to the surface. She was back in one of the worst of times – the autumn of 1939.

The shelling of the City by the German army had been light and little damage had been done. It was more in the nature of a warning, and knowing that armed resistance was hopeless, the Czechoslovak authorities had capitulated. Promised help from the West had not materialised; the German leader had said it was his last demand in Europe, and the Czech people had been abandoned to their fate.

The immediate measures imposed by the German occupiers had affected everyone. Within one week the traffic system had been changed from driving on the left to driving on the right – thus conforming to German pattern and vehicles. But it was more than a convenience for the Germans; it affected every Czech man, woman and child, and there was no more effective way of imposing their domination completely without bloodshed.

Then they had required all businesses – public and private – to use German as the first language. Tereza had no problem with this as her German was at the least adequate, but it was the third measure which enraged her – their treatment of the large Jewish population of the city.

She remembered vividly the walk to Mostecká Street one crisp autumn morning. The leaves were turning all gold and red, and some were already falling; the nights were drawing in but the mornings often clear and bright. She had just crossed the road toward the tram stop when she saw, shuffling towards her in the gutter, the figure of an old man. He wore a long coat and a hat the brim of which was pulled down to hide as much of his face as possible. But this was no tramp; as they drew closer Tereza saw the yellow star standing out on his coat. She slowed and stopped: the old man looked up.

"Shimon!" she exclaimed, "you look ... so cold."

She slipped her arm through his and started to walk a few steps back with him. Looking intently at the face of this old family friend, she did not see the German soldiers standing in her way until the last minute.

"I wouldn't do that," said one of the soldiers.

"You might finish up where he's going," joked another.

One of them took her roughly by the shoulders and turned her round. "You get on your way and we won't ask your name this time." Then he added in her ear, "I don't forget faces, mind!" and he slapped her backside hard to help her on her way.

Tereza, her face scarlet, ran. She did not look back. She heard the soldiers abusing the old man and the sound of blows.

She never saw Shimon again.

They first met early in 1942.

Tereza then worked for Antonín, an elderly, grizzled fellow who ran the City's Housing Department efficiently and was reckoned something of a martinet by those who did not see him at close quarters. But she knew, as did others who worked in that same office, that Antonín's bite was reserved solely for the slothful and lazy.

It was late one morning when the stranger first entered the office; a solid man in his mid-twenties, deep-chested, with a full head of black hair thrown back and a cheerful grin. He didn't knock, just came straight in, kicked the door shut and marched up to Antonín, hand outstretched.

Stanislav as he appeared about 1942.

"I'm Stanislav. Messenger. Attached to this floor and at your service.!"

Antonín put his pencil down and took the proffered hand. A pause, then looking straight at his visitor he rasped, "I didn't ask for a messenger. I have no messages, and when I have I shall use the usual channels."

Work stopped, heads swivelled and Tereza saw Stanislav looking straight at her. For a brief moment Tereza experienced a consternation she had never felt before; she gripped her chair quite tightly. Stanislav perched on the edge of Antonín's desk, continuing to look at Tereza while saying to no one in particular, "I am your usual channel from now on."

He eased himself off the desk, turned towards the door and then added slowly and deliberately, "By Order of the German Army." They all watched the door close behind him. None of the women in the office moved or spoke. Antonín, recognising a military man when he saw one, broke the silence. Very quietly, he said, "No, he is not German, nor is he working for the Germans. Just in case you are unaware, the German authorities have demobilised our military forces into civic works and buildings as civilian personnel. Though they were disarmed within a few weeks of the invasion, they are still viewed as a threat to the occupying army – thus the policy of dispersal. As for that young man, just remember he would much rather be fighting the Germans than enduring the humiliation of menial tasks in the Housing Department. Treat him civilly and above all, don't ask him questions."

There was a shuffling, a clearing of throats, a muffled, "Yes, Sir."

"Right, let's get back to work."

Antonín picked up his pencil, then stared at it for a moment. "The young devil! He's taken my good pencil and left me this little chewed stub!"

He rushed to the door and called down the corridor, "Hey, you! Stanislav! Come back with my pencil!"

But Stanislav was nowhere to be seen.

And Tereza realised she was blushing.

That evening, after supper, Tereza busied herself heating the iron while Marie and her Grandmother sat by the big china stove. Ostensibly, Marie was reading out loud from one of her Grandmother's favourite books, but it was much more of a question and answer and giggle session. Tereza smiled, tested the iron and set about the pile of washing that had dried out in the garden behind the flats during the day. One of Marie's school shirts was the first garment.

And so she remembered ironing Stanislav's shirts.

As she smoothed out a sleeve and the cuff, memories of her brief domestic life with her husband came racing back. She remembered even their conversation the first time she was able to speak to Stanislav on her own. Every day he would come into the office and do whatever jobs were to hand. Quite early on, he asked Antonín if he would like hooks put on the back of the office door.

"Somewhere for you to hang your coat."

"But I hang my coat on that stand over there."

"And half the time the stand falls over because people have taken the screws out for other jobs. Now if I put the hooks on the back of the door with the three screws that remain in the stand, I can take the bits of the stand back to stores and draw a new one."

"But if you've put hooks on the door we won't want another stand."

"No, but the Head of Cleansing does, and I can swap it for that empty two-drawer filing cabinet of his which would take all the extra paperwork you've been grumbling about recently."

That clinched it. Antonín lapsed into growl mode and told Stanislav to get on with it.

That day, Tereza worked on into the lunch break to finish a particular job. She was startled by Stanislav suddenly slipping quietly into the room, and aware immediately by the expression on his face that he expected the office to be empty. He leant back against the door.

"Now," he said hesitantly, "you're Tereza. Is that right?"

"Yes, indeed," she smiled back.

"How long have you worked here?"

"Just on five years."

"Do you like it?"

Odd question, she thought. "It's a job, like any other. I am paid, and I spend most winter days inside in the warm."

Stanislav thought for a moment, then advancing into the middle of the room, asked,

"Do you ever have to go out – in your job, I mean?"

"Oh, yes, occasionally I have to see what's happening to some of the City property, or to settle queries with tenants."

"Well, tell me next time you have to go out. Would you mind if I came with you?"

She would be delighted, but she didn't put it quite as strongly as that. Excusing herself, she rushed out of the office and down to the canteen.

When Antonín returned, he noticed that the old coat stand was gone and there were three brass hooks on the back of the door.

What he did not notice was that a file was missing. It related to a block of flats in a city suburb, some of whose occupants were of particular interest to one of Stanislav's former military colleagues.

It was the morning of 27th May,1942, a morning much like any other in the beleaguered city – that is until Stanislav breezed into Antonín's office shortly before 11 o'clock. He gave his usual cheery greeting to the girls, and then deposited a fat file in front of Antonín.

"This is the one you sent for, but I think you ought to look at a new entry."

He moved round the desk and opened the file.

Then he whispered in Antonín's ear, "There has been an assassination attempt on our Reichsprotektor, Heydrich. It is not yet known whether it was successful."

"Good God! When?"

"About an hour ago. I will let you know when I have more news. In the meantime, say nothing to your staff but think of jobs you could send them out on."

Stanislav straightened up. "I'll call back for the file later," he announced clearly, and was gone.

Antonín gazed at the documents in front of him, but his mind was racing ahead. Whether the hated Heydrich lived or died, there were bound to be reprisals. He ran his hands through his greying hair and looked round the room. How many of us, he wondered, are going to survive? Not for a moment did he doubt that eventually they would be free again, but what was the price they would have to pay? ... how long would it be? ... how many lives would it cost?

He shut the file and pushed it to one side. '... jobs you could send them out on ...' Stanislav had said. Just what that meant he was not sure, but there was a survey he wanted done which could occupy three of them; now, how to employ the other two?

Perhaps they could start estimating for that renovation over at ... no, no, the City treasurer would never grant ... and then he was not sure Stanislav meant that. If Heydrich was dead there would be immediate reprisals ... better not send them out at all.

He couldn't concentrate ... when the door opened again and Stanislav shut it quickly behind him, an hour had passed.

"Finished with that?" and he was alongside Antonín, fussing with the file. Realising that he was not going to go round and tease them, the girls turned back reluctantly to their work.

Stanislav whispered, "He's been taken to hospital; he was wounded but we don't know how badly – in fact we don't know whether he's still alive. Our two men got away though one was certainly hurt. The Germans will declare martial law; any possible suspect will be taken in and they won't waste time asking questions.. I suggest you get your staff home – now."

Antonín cleared his throat. Stanislav turned and looked directly at Tereza. Antonín spoke.

"Listen, please. There has been an attempt on the life of Reinhard Heydrich. You are all to go home; don't talk to anyone – plead illness if you are stopped. Listen to your wireless tonight, and report in again in the morning. And remember to have all the necessary papers – identity card; your work permit; ration card; tobacco card, and driving licence if you have one. Now go – one at a time."

Heydrich died a week later. He was an SS man; reprisals were swift and extreme.

The Czech Resistance men, trained in England and parachuted in, were betrayed and committed suicide after a gun battle with the SS.

All Czechs already in German hands, known or suspected of connections with Obrana Naroda (Defence of the Nation) were shot. In the pocket of one – actually an SOE agent – was a scrap of paper with the word 'Lidice' written on it. Though the village had no link whatsoever with the assassination, it was surrounded; every man, woman and child rounded up, the men were shot; the women and children sent to concentration camps and the village razed to the ground. The site was ploughed up.

The name 'Lidice' rang round the world.

It was some months later when Tereza was out on a task for Antonín that she felt his hands on her shoulders first, and then quietly in her ear, "I'm on escort duty this morning."

"Thank you," she said. "Sorry I couldn't let you know. It was an early call."

The tram was crowded. They dated their tickets and he made sure she had a seat while he stood close by. Throughout the journey, he appeared to be looking for something or someone – first in the tram itself, then out on the streets. She watched him, dressed this time in an anonymous raincoat, trilby, grey trousers, black shoes.

No smile this morning, his face set hard in a way she had not seen before. Oh! How she wanted to ask questions of this man! She was sure there was much more to him than the cheerful, breezy fellow who greeted the office every morning. Oh, yes, much more … but then back came Antonín's warning, "… above all, don't ask him questions."

At the stop before theirs, two German soldiers boarded the tram. Stanislav hung from a strap and looked at his shoes until he felt the tram slow down. As soon as it stopped, he took Tereza's hand and they were out in the fresh air.

Tereza

'... raincoat, trilby, grey trousers, black shoes.'

She was glad of his company. The tenant she had to question was an awkward old man who, seeing they had sent a woman to ask for the back rent, could lapse into his cantankerous mood and the job would take ages with no guarantee of ultimate success.

Not so that morning. At the first sign of hesitation, Stanislav produced something out of his pocket. Tereza caught the merest glimpse of his movement, but whatever he held in his hand produced the desired effect. The back rent was quickly forthcoming.

They walked down past Nerudová Street, and then taking her arm Stanislav guided her along a sidestreet with which she was unfamiliar. Shortly, he stopped and said, "Coffee?" and added under his breath, "... or what passes for coffee."

Not waiting for an answer he opened a small shop door, down a few stone steps and into what might have been a basement at some time. The ceiling was stone, arched over in segments like ceilings Tereza knew in much larger, grander buildings. This was Old Town, medieval; a place of wonder but on an intimate scale. A small fountain gushed out of one wall into a trough with plants and ferns growing. Her shoes sounded on the stone floor.

As they entered a young girl appeared from a kitchen at the back of the shop and stood at the counter. Stanislav ordered, and then added, "Tell your father he has a customer."

The shop was deserted. They sat at a table near the fountain and had just settled when a tall, middle-aged man appeared in the kitchen doorway. He and Stanislav clearly knew each other but no words passed, merely a look and a nod.

The coffee arrived and they talked about the office ... the latest gossip ... trivia.

Then Stanislav leaned forward and said, "Tell me about your Uncle."

There was no need to ask what Uncle he meant but she hesitated, not knowing quite what she ought to say.

"What have you heard?" he asked gently.

"Simply that he has been arrested by the Germans and taken to the camp at Terežin for questioning." She wondered how much he knew. "He was in the Army, a Major stationed at Plzeň."

"Tell me about him."

"Well, he's my mother's eldest sister's husband ... joined the Army straight from school. A professional soldier."

Tereza paused for some moments. Then drawing a deep breath, "I mean it's not as if he was a Communist, or a gipsy, or the kind of man they've been arresting. And he's certainly not Jewish! We just can't understand why they've taken him." She was on the verge of tears.

Stanislav took her hands in his over the table. "Finish your coffee," he said quietly, "we don't want Antonín coming to look for you." And then another under-the-breath remark, "Not that he would look for you here, I hope."

When she finally reached the City Council building, opened the office door and reported success in her task, Antonín looked at her and commented dryly, "I must send you on more jobs like that. Judging by your colour they seem to do you good."

It was quite uncanny.

Over the weeks and months that followed, whenever Tereza was sent out on Housing Department business – whether it was a brief enquiry or an all-day job supervising a tenancy change – Stanislav seemed to have pre-knowledge and would appear. Sometimes he would join her for several hours; on other occasions it was simply a passing in the street without even recognition. She began to look for him, knowing he was there somewhere; it was like having a guardian angel and she was infinitely grateful.

Life had become progressively worse after the assassination of Heydrich. There had been rationing of food within the first few weeks of the invasion; now this was extended to articles of clothing while simple shortages effectively rationed many other kinds of goods. Soap and toiletries were especially difficult to get and though Tereza never asked, Stanislav helped from time to time with small items slipped unobtrusively into her pocket while they were walking. A loaf of bread or a tiny packet of sugar appeared at the bottom of her bag when she unpacked in the evening.

More sinister was the steady infiltration of German military and civil personnel into positions of power and influence. Czechoslovak nationals who resisted in action or word usually disappeared, their names subsequently appearing in the lists on public buildings and in newspapers as 'traitors' who had been executed.

One morning Stanislav and Antonín had their heads close together for several minutes before Stanislav picked up the same pile of papers which he had brought and quietly left the office.

Antonín found a large map of the City and spread it on his desk. "I want you all to gather round and study this map," he said to his little band of assistants.

"Now don't look at me. Keep your heads down and look at the map. In case anyone peers through the glass panels I may point at the map from time to time; follow my finger, but listen to what I have to say." He paused until satisfied that they were all together.

"We shall get a visit from a woman who will not give her name but say she is acting on behalf of the Commissar (Mayor), and is looking for documents which have gone astray. She will use this excuse to search this office thoroughly. She is German. Before she gets here – and she could come at any time – go through your desks, drawers, lockers, handbags, coat pockets and remove anything that could be remotely construed as anti-German. From now on, I cannot help you if she finds anything she regards as suspicious. Furthermore, while she is in the room, or the vicinity of this room, we all speak German. Karel, I know you are finding it difficult, but mumble, chatter as best you can. Not a word of Czech, mind. You will recognise her easily..." and he finished with a detailed description of the woman in question.

Tereza caught the tram home that night with a heavy heart. She had thought about the spy in the building; knew that the information had come from Stanislav, but... how had he known? Rumours were rife; each day brought its crop, but whatever information Stanislav gave seemed to be genuine. How was he so well informed?

She got off the tram and he materialised out of the shadows. He slipped his arm through hers and they walked at a steady pace in the way he had taught her.

Walk close to the wall. Keep your head down but watch everything carefully. Never draw attention to yourself whatever the circumstances.

When vehicles passed he whispered in her ear, "I have news of your Uncle. It is bad, I'm afraid. He has been moved to Berlin for further interrogation."

"Then we shall not see him again," said Tereza, looking straight ahead.

"It is unlikely," conceded Stanislav, as gently as he could.

They walked on in silence until they came to the archway over the entrance to Tereza's flat. Up the slope to the doorway, where she turned and he placed his hands on her shoulders. From the road, it looked like lovers kissing goodnight; indeed his lips brushed gently against her cheek but in her ear he whispered, "You must be brave. Just trust me. Now go in and lock the door."

Tereza held him; kissed him full on the lips... and then he was gone.

Their courtship – for that was what it had now become – was unorthodox by normal standards. But this was war: Prague was an occupied city and the German military, and to some extent the civil authorities, had it in an iron grip.

No one felt safe; words and actions had always to be thought out first.

On the bedroom dresser was a small piece of pottery which Tereza had been given as a child. It consisted of three monkeys, the first had its paws over its eyes, the second had its paws over its ears, the third over its mouth. The legend below read, "See no evil, hear no evil, speak no evil."

At first Tereza thought this a splendid example for a child; later she came to see it as a symbol of the way she had to survive as an adult. It was not that she had to see no evil for that was always there in the way so many of the city's people were treated, no, rather it was a reminder that you heard nothing; saw nothing and kept your mouth shut.

This made a romance difficult, for Tereza wanted to sing and dance and show off this man who had broken into her life but she knew it to be an impossibility. To begin with, he was ex-military which made him a marked man with the occupying forces, but there was something else – this unofficial knowledge which he possessed; the excessive care he took of her and his reluctance to give other than minimal information about himself. There was only one explanation and that was that he was involved in a Resistance or Escape movement.

If she had made a correct guess she never mentioned it, nor her suspicion that the coffee shop near Nerudová Street was some sort of meeting place or communication post. Stanislav slipped in through the shop door one evening just as it was closing. The tall man whom Tereza had seen briefly before, greeted Stanislav and led him into the deserted kitchen.

"That Major from Plžen you're interested in."

"Yes, any news?"

"Our contact in Berlin reports that the Major was executed last week. Apparently someone broke and linked him to the Poland escape. No doubt they'll publish it: it'll be 'Treason, Sedition' – that sort of thing. Better tell your lady before she sees it in print."

"You sure he's got this right?"

"He's been reliable so far. I think you have to accept it."

Stanislav left by the rear entrance.

The news of her Uncle's death did not surprise Tereza; it came more as a confirmation of what she had already assumed in her mind. It was of a pattern with events that followed over the months and years not just in the city but over the country as a whole. As the war progressed, it began to turn against the Axis powers. There was the German retreat from Russia, the Allied invasion of

Tereza

Tereza on Charles Bridge in her beloved Prague.

France and the Low Countries, and the bitter fighting northwards in Italy. But there was no diminution of oppression and cruelty in the occupied territories of central Europe. There was continued transportation of the Jewish peoples, and for the Czechoslovaks who remained desperate shortages of food and supplies.

It was one evening shortly before Christmas 1944. She had packed away the work of the day and was preparing for the journey home; most of her friends had left, Antonín spread the baize cloth over his desk top and locked his drawers. Tereza took her coat from the brass hook and put it on – she would be glad of its warmth even in its now threadbare condition in the cold of the evening. She reached into the large side pockets for her gloves and scarf, tying the latter firmly round her head. First one glove, then the other. She turned to bid Antonín goodnight when she realised that there was a small piece of paper in her right hand glove.

Mystified, she drew it out. In pencil, in capital letters, was the message, "Do not ask for me. Do not look for me. It will not be long now – wait for me. S"

Horrified, she stood stock still, gazing at the scrap of paper.

At the Yalta Conference early in 1945, Roosevelt, Churchill and Stalin agreed upon the military strategy to bring about the final collapse of Hitler and the Nazi regime. This included the areas of occupation by American, British and Russian Forces, and it was agreed that Allied armies should relieve Czechoslovakia.

However, by April 1945, the Yalta Agreement had been broken or disregarded by the Russians in every important case which had, at that time, been put to the test of action.

While it was by no means impossible for Eisenhower's armies to reach Prague, the Western powers, disturbed by these political developments, re-directed their military efforts to the race for Berlin. Czechoslovakia was left to the Russians who entered Prague on 5th May 1945, aided by the Czech Revolutionary Army or Underground Movement, of which Stanislav was a Member. The day became known as the May Uprising. There had been little resistance from the occupying German Forces who were in the process of withdrawing to the rugged area of Western Austria and Southern Bavaria.

Thus the liberation became a sphere of influence and the pattern of political domination was set for many years to come.

III

Stanislav

(Compiled from Military records)

Born: 2 May 1916 at Domažlice, about 100 miles south west of Prague near the border with Germany.

In October 1936, he joined the Czechoslovak Army (previous occupation listed as 'Student') and was posted to the School for Officers of the Air Force at Prostějov. After basic training, he was transferred to the Military Academy at Hranice and was commissioned as a Lieutenant of the Air Force in August 1938.

Stanislav in the uniform of Captain, Czechoslovak Air Force.

He joined the Reserve Flight of the 1st Air Regiment, and six weeks later was transferred to the 3rd Observer Flight at Milovice. But in January 1939 he was back at Prostějov on an accelerated Course for Junior Officers.

Following the German occupation, the Czechoslovak Air Force was demobilised in March 1939 and in September Stanislav was declared a civilian and assigned to the staff of the Mayor of Prague for 'administrative and financial duties'. Just where he worked between that date and his arrival at the offices of the City Housing department in 1942 is not known.

Nor is it clear just when he joined the Revolutionary Military Brigade (otherwise known as the Underground Movement). Nor do we know precisely when this clandestine movement – controlled for most of its existence by Czech nationals lead by František Moravec working from London – was sufficiently confident, well-equipped and led to become organised on military lines in Prague itself. Suffice to say that Stanislav probably joined in 1944 or early 1945: he was certainly involved in the Uprising on 5th May 1945.

On 26th May 1945, Stanislav joined the re-established Czechoslovak Army, and was posted to the Ministry of National Defence Headquarters of the Air Force in Prague. In September 1945, he was sent on a Navigation Course prior to a posting to No 311 Squadron, part of the 24th Air Regiment stationed at Plzeň.

Captain Stanislav Zidlický about to board Mosquito. Aircraft in background displays Czech roundels and identification marks'.

By May 1946, Stanislav had been promoted to Captain and 311 Squadron arrived in England to convert onto De Havilland Mosquito aircraft. The Course was completed in two months and new aircraft, collected from the factory at Hatfield, were flown back to Kbely airfield on the outskirts of Prague.

In July 1946, he was appointed Adjutant to the Commanding Officer of the 24th Air Regiment. His flying duties were not neglected, however, for he was back with his Squadron in December for further transfer flights of Mosquito aircraft from Hatfield to Kbely.

A widening experience for an able Officer followed. From New Year's Day 1947, he became an Instructor at the Air Force School of N.C.O's at Budějovice. By late May though, Stanislav was back in the air and a third visit to England took place from the 15th to the 21st of May.

There followed a stable period with his Squadron during which he qualified as a Navigator (February 1948), and was promoted to Štábní Kapitán (April 1948), the equivalent of the RAF Squadron Leader.

Medal found in Stanislav's possession after his death. The ribbon reads 'Headquarters Revolutionary Army Prague 5'. 'Bartoš' was the name of a First World War hero and the Unit was named after him.

The final entry in his Record reads, "Died in air crash during military duties, Kvaštov, in district of Sedlčany. 4th March 1949"

IV

Tereza and Stanislav

PRAGUE

They were re-united after the Prague Uprising in May 1945 and something like

Stanislav and Tereza, sometime between May 1945 and March 1949

a normal courtship followed.

The marriage ceremony.

Tereza and Stanislav were married in Prague on 21st December 1948, and moved into a maisonette in Leningradská Ulice.

Stanislav and Tereza after their wedding.

The crash site near Kvaštov.

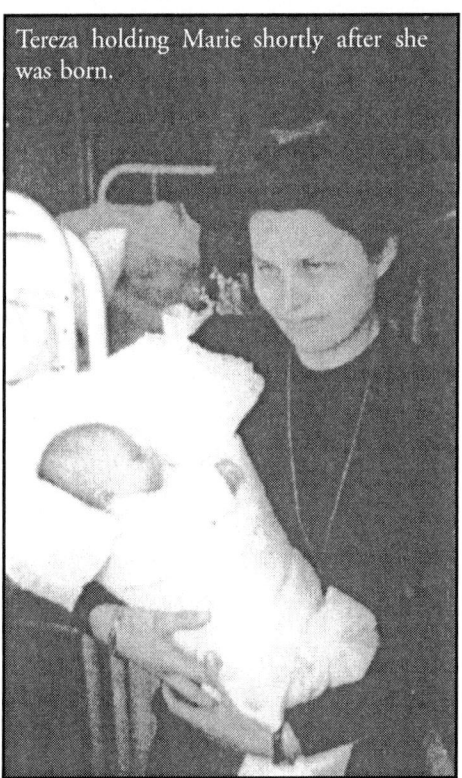

Tereza holding Marie shortly after she was born.

Stanislav and his crew member were killed in a flying accident on 4th March 1949, the aircraft coming down in a wooded area near Kvaštov. It has not been possible to discover the cause of the accident.

A daughter, Marie, was born on 18th September 1949.

V

Tereza and Marie

PRAGUE. 1957
The Communist Party came to power in Czechoslovakia on 27th February 1948.

"Enter," grunted the Commissar in response to the timid knock. He did not look up until he had heard the door open and shut again quietly, and then counted to twenty.

"Ah, Vladimír Roubíček, I sent for you."

Vladimír stood just inside the spacious room, waiting. He was one of nature's unfortunates who, despite all efforts to appear neat and smart, was doomed to present himself as a tall and willowy shrub in need of pruning. In vain would he claim to have combed his hair that morning; to have positioned his tie in line with his chin, or to have searched for buttons for his shirt cuffs which now protruded out of control from his jacket sleeves. His normal cheerful manner was subdued as he obeyed the Commissar's gesture to approach.

"You have made it clear in many recent Reports that you need assistance in the Housing Department," the Commissar began in ponderous tone. "To demonstrate that we in the ... mmm ... higher echelons of management are aware of the many problems faced by those who work for the Mayor and City Corporation, I have good news for you."

"Thank you, Commissar," breathed Vladimír.

"You are to have an assistant. Her name is Tereza Židlická and she will report to your office next week."

"Thank you, Commissar," repeated Vladimír, a shade too enthusiastically.

"And should you feel inclined to throw your weight about and bully the lady, I can inform you that she has more experience in the Housing Department than you!"

The Commissar consulted the file in front of him. "Yes, she started in 1937 and worked until her marriage in 1948. Before the Revolution of course, but I imagine she will know more about the problems and how to solve them than you have learnt in the ... how long have you worked here?"

For the first time in the interview, the Commissar looked up directly at Vladimír. What he saw did not please him.

"Just five years, Commissar."

"Yes, I am sure she will know more about the workings of the Department than you. Now perhaps we may expect some degree of efficiency from Housing.

You may go, Vladimír Roubíček, and return via the washroom. Tidy yourself up, otherwise you may be working as the lady's assistant the week after next!"

Vladimír left quietly, and looked in at the Commissar's pretty secretary, Jana. From the expression on her face as she fought her typewriter, this was not the moment to ask a favour. He walked the tedious way back along the grey corridors, down the grey staircases until he reached the ground floor office and flung himself into the swivel chair. The noise of his return prompted movement in the adjoining office and then young Novák's head appeared round the door.

"Ah, there you are, Vladimír … "

"Go away," responded Vladimír ungraciously.

"Very well," said Novák rather truculently. "Don't forget that Josef Janáček is coming to see you in half an hour." Novák banged the door shut and returned to his rabbit hutch.

Vladimír groaned. Josef Janáček was Head of Supplies and was almost certainly going to grill him about that latest Requisition for new furniture. Janáček was a devoted member of the Party – nothing wrong with that – but trying to wrest supplies out of Supplies was very hard work indeed.

And Vladimír felt limp after his interview with the Commissar. Pleased to have some help at last and delighted to think that the Higher Echelons at last recognised the vital needs of the Housing Department, yet the sound of his new assistant was not entirely to his liking. If she had started work with Housing back in 1937 – some twenty years ago – then she was not the young and pretty kind for which he had hoped. Married, too; perhaps she was the bossy sort who would try to take over and run the Department just when he seemed to have made his mark and been noticed. There was only one thing for it he decided, he must get hold of his new assistant's file from the Commissar's office. He was considering various options for Jana when the door opened and the bulky frame of Janáček appeared.

"Ah, Vladimír Roubíček … " For the second time that morning, the formal phrase frightened the life out of him.

It was two days later that Vladimír again walked from the rarefied fifth floor observing the first rule for those who had no business to be there: *Always carry a file or two and walk purposefully.* It had cost him a small jar of genuine coffee, and even with that generous back-hander Jana had refused to pass the file herself. "Come and fetch it yourself, Vladimír Roubíček, if you want it so badly."

'Little minx,' he thought to himself, 'getting ideas above herself,' but it was exactly where she said it would be, sandwiched between his own 'Housing – Occupation percentage figures' and a file of blank paper. He had simply picked up all three files and left quickly. Now back in his own office he considered his next move. Housing Department files were buff, Personnel files were bright blue, and at his level he had no authority to carry one – let alone open and read it.

'What if someone should come in? A blue file on my desk ... no, can't risk it ... Take it home in the brief case? ... no, bound to be an Exit Inspection on the evening when there is something to hide. Only one thing for it.'

Still carrying the three files, Vladimír sought sanctuary. Gently, he pushed open the door and peered round. Empty! It was only when he had slid the bolt on the least offensive lavatory that he sighed with relief, sat down and looked at the blue file.

In the Supplies Department, Josef Janáček called his most junior assistant, Novák, into his office.

"I believe," Janáček observed quietly, "that you are a ... what shall I say ... near neighbour of the Head of Housing Department, Vladimír Roubíček. Is that correct?"

"Yes," replied Novák cautiously, "I live in the next street."

"And would I be right in assuming that you travel to and from work together?"

"Yes ... that is, when circumstances permit, ... of course."

"Of course. And despite your being ... what shall I say ... just a few years younger, you must know our comrade well."

Immediately, Novák sensed danger. He had given Janáček grounds for this supposition, yet he could not see where this questioning about a comrade was leading. He paused to consider options. Janáček still could not understand why such a comparatively younger man as Roubíček, walking haystack that he was, had gained such swift promotion to lead a Municipal Department. Now Housing was to have an assistant while he, Janáček, mature and experienced, had no increase in his allocation. It was not fair; it was not reasonable; it needed investigation.

"Well, Novák?"

"We all know each other on the surface, Comrade Janáček; few of us know each other well. That is how I am with Comrade Roubíček."

Janáček sighed. "Do you know why he missed the last Party meeting?"

"No, Comrade Janáček," Novák lied.

"You may go, Novák."

Aware that Roubíček would soon be advised of the conversation which had just taken place, Janáček resolved that he needed to take Roubíček's loyalty in hand. A walk in the park might be a suitable start.

Vladimír looked at the blue file. Down the right hand edge was her name, Tereza, in large printed letters, the maiden name *'Koksteinová'* crossed out by hand and her married name substituted. Her national identity number ran along the top. Vladimír opened it.

There was a bunch of periodic Report Forms, commenting on such qualities as diligence, competence, appearance; Courses attended and qualifications gained. The last of these Forms was different in layout and included a large space to be completed by the Political Officer for the Department. Vladimír riffed quickly through and found what he was looking for – the Personal Details Form. Tattered from twenty years in the file, the original typescript faint and old-fashioned, he made out that she had been born in Prague in 1914 and did a quick mental calculation. Reading on, he learnt that her father had been killed in 1917, and that she was an only child.

Her address had been altered, but the original was still visible. He knew the district – one of the poorer quarters of the old town – though the exact location escaped him. He knew the schools she had attended; that she had remained in education until 19 surprised him. 'Bright child from a poor home' was his conclusion, especially when under 'Languages' was the entry 'German, French, Latin' and a later hand-written entry 'Russian'.

His concentration was suddenly broken by the opening of the washroom door. Heavy footsteps lead in the direction of the urinals, a pause, then the ripe sound of breaking wind followed by a grunt of relief. A few moments later, footsteps and the sound of the door opening and shutting.

Vladimír had not moved a muscle. Now, alone again, he let the Report Forms slip over one by one as he glanced through them. Tereza had, it appeared, been a diligent and hard-working employee; clean and neat, but not considered suitable for promotion.

Almost at the end, his eyes widened at the sight of purple ink. He had heard that in some countries, purple was the colour of royalty; not here. A purple entry was a warning – its use restricted to Political Officers. Her marriage was recorded, dated December 1948, to an Officer in the Air Force. There it was cross-referenced to another file – presumably his – and then in the same hand a single word and date, *Deceased 03.49*

'So the lady is a widow' registered Vladimír's sub-conscious.

Finally, pinned to the top of the papers, was a single sheet with the entry in the Commissar's hand, 'Now considered suitable for re-employment; low-grade only'. It was dated from the previous week in May 1957.

Vladimír closed the file and restored it between the two buff ones. He had not heard anyone else enter the washroom but just in case he rustled his clothing and hit the flush button. This produced encouraging sounds but no water.

He was still no wiser about Tereza's fall from political grace. It must have been very early on in the Communist regime and not desperately serious for here she was back in State employment, but 'Low-grade only', – they were taking no chances.

Emerging, he walked smartly back to his own department. No sooner had he shut the door than it opened again.

"Meet me in the washroom in two minutes," whispered Novák and was gone.

Vladimír wondered why life had suddenly become so complicated.

Tereza gazed round the office she had left many years before. Old Antonín's desk was where it had been but now it was littered with papers, files, the remnants of yesterday's lunch, a magazine or two. Where her old desk had been, stood a modern table piled high with office junk. 'We must clear this for you,' enthused Vladimír, intent on giving the impression of an efficient manager.

"Do you have any other staff working for you?" asked Tereza with sinking heart.

"Oh, yes," said Vladimír, "I have a man who does all the legwork for me. Looks after the properties and sorts out the problems on the ground. Leaves me clear to cope with the paperwork." He rubbed his hands together in satisfaction at this claim but then spoilt it by adding, "Of course, I have to share him with other departments."

He groaned inwardly. ('If only I knew when to stop!') But Tereza had turned and he heard her exclaim, "Oh, there's still one brass hook on the back of the door ..."

Vladimír thought it a very odd thing to say.

It took the rest of the morning to sort out and agree on Tereza's share of the work. He did not want to focus too sharply on his mid-day break: he had been 'invited' to join his fellow Head of Department, Josef Janáček, for a walk in the park.

The Communist Party came to power in Czechoslovakia on 27th February 1948.

President Beneš was deposed and a new Government installed. There was one rather surprising inclusion though. Jan Masaryk, who had staunchly opposed the Communists, was retained as Foreign Minister. This was seen as an enlightened move and applauded by many of an older generation, for he was the son of the former – and much revered – President Masaryk.

It was unfortunate therefore, that on the 10th March 1948, Jan Masaryk slipped and fell from the balcony outside a first floor window of the government building. He died of his injuries.

In the early years of the regime, there was a general welcome – indeed in some quarters enthusiasm – for the communist philosophy. Soviet values commanded belief – in theory, and many thought their practitioners could not be worse than the German occupiers. Most of those in authority were Czechoslovaks who had been trained in Russia; some were Jews who had survived the camps – all were committed to the basic principle that the end justifies the means.

Or as Janáček put it to Vladimír as they walked in the Spring sunshine, "That is, and remains the only rule of political ethics. Surely you are not giving one moment's consideration to the concept that the individual is sacrosanct?

"Good heavens, no!"

Janáček stopped dead in his tracks. He was right; this young man was slipping. "You see, your speech is a reflection of your thinking. Where did you get that expression from?"

"I didn't mean it literally, Comrade. Don't take me up like that," Vladimír pleaded indignantly.

"I don't approve of mixing ideologies, even in friendly and of course enlightened conversations such as this," retorted Janáček, as they continued their stroll. "Always remember what you have been taught, that there are only two basic political concepts and that they are at opposite ends of the spectrum. Over in the so-called free Western countries, they would have us believe that their political ethic is humane and derives from the Christian principle that the value of individual life is paramount. The rules of arithmetic do not apply to human units. That is nonsense, is it not?"

"Yes, of course, Comrade." Vladimír began perspiring.

"Can you name one country that has Christianity as a state religion and has really followed a Christian political policy?"

"No, Comrade."

"It is we who are truly free because we start from the opposite principle that the collective aim justifies all means, and once we have that clear in our minds then we are free to demand that the interests of the individual be subordinate to the interests of the community. We must work at this, Comrade Roubíček, we must work at this."

"Yes, I agree entirely, but … (Vladimír paused; this was a point at which he must stop; he had learnt something from the lecture. He glanced at his watch) … but we should be returning to our daily work, Comrade."

He was astonished at how the office had changed in so short a time. It appeared, well, tidy. Tereza had cleared her allocated table and set out pads of paper, rulers, pencils and so forth. She stood studying a map of the city which she had fixed to the wall behind her table.

It was several weeks later that Vladimír and Novák were able to spend a few minutes of the Mayor's time chatting together.

"She's very quiet, but good … efficient."

Novák grinned, "And too old for you!"

"I am surprised," retorted Vladimír loftily, "that you should bracket us together in such terms. It is true that I am still single and … perhaps … looking to settle down now, but …"

Novák grinned wider.

"… to suggest that the City Hall is the only source for a possible …"

"And much too public!" chortled Novák. "In any case, she's out of your class."

Vladimír was about to issue an instant denial when he realised that he could reveal knowing more about Tereza than a Grade 8 clerk (albeit temporary Head of Department) had any right to know. Resorting to mock violence, he bundled Novák out of his office.

Pausing only to pick up a sandwich from the paper packet on his desk, he strolled to the back of the room and looked through the small, grimy glass partition which overlooked the public interview hall. At the back, a roped-off area held the throng of those who had – or purported to have – business with one of the Council's Departments. In the foreground were a number of interview booths. When one became vacant, an official lifted the rope and permitted someone who had shown generosity to stoop beneath and rush to the empty booth. Most had waited hours.

Vladimír surveyed the scene, wiped his fingers on the front of his pullover and spotted Tereza listening to a young woman in her early twenties. Yes, he thought to himself, she is good; she listens well – she even gives the impression of being mildly interested. He knew perfectly well that was a talent he lacked totally and so as often as not it was Tereza who was despatched to the interview room.

On this occasion, having concluded her business, Tereza put her head round the office door and announced that she was off to the Registrar's department. Vladimír could not leave well alone. Tereza had acted correctly, informing him of her intended whereabouts but he had to act the boss. Apart from demonstrating his superior rank, he was curious.

"What do you need to know from them?"

"It could be that there's an available flat in the Vysočany area, and I need to know."

"Nonsense! There's never a vacant flat there. Always full of old men and women and hordes of children. Don't waste your time."

Tereza sighed. "I didn't say 'vacant' Comrade; I said 'available'."

Vladimír looked completely blank; he hadn't really listened; hadn't noticed.

Tereza came in and shut the door. "You see, often when the named tenant dies the son or daughter moves in and takes over. Only they don't tell us; that would mean having to wait their turn for accommodation because we would offer the flat to the next on the list. So the rent continues to be paid; signatures are forged, the maintenance men are bribed and neighbours connive as they would probably wish to do the same thing when their time comes. But the death has to be registered, otherwise there's no funeral. However, as the Registrar's Department never communicate, I have to check with them whether any of our tenants in that area has died within the last year. That is why I am going to the Registrar's department."

She turned and slipped out, closing the door quietly.

Vladimír stared after her.

They were walking in the park again. Josef Janáček had decided to take his comrade under his wing; partly through a genuine desire to ensure his return to the ideological fold, and partly to try to understand why this younger man had risen to his present baffling height in the Mayor's employ.

It was not a pleasant experience for Vladimír, for whom the more material aspects of life were more enticing than political theory. It was a delightful summer's day, the sun hot and they were not the only pair walking off their lunch. Janáček was in full flow.

"We seem to be faced with a pendulum movement in history, swinging from absolutism to democracy, from democracy back to absolute dictatorship."

Vladimír removed his jacket and swung it over his shoulder.

"The amount of political freedom which a people may attain and keep, depends on the degree of its political maturity. The aforementioned pendulum motion ... "

Vladimír smiled happily at two young girls as they passed. They smiled back, laughing and giggling behind Vladimír's back.

"... seems to indicate that the political maturing of the masses does not follow a continuous rising curve, as does the growing up of an individual, ... "

A group of young men sat on the grass, relaxing, watching the world go by. Vladimír wished he too was a spectator. He glanced furtively at his watch.

"... but that it is governed by more complicated laws. The maturity of the masses lies in their capacity to recognise their own self-interests."

"We really should be making for the gate, Comrade," pleaded Vladimír, "though I have found your views most interesting."

Janáček turned his gaze full on Vladimír. Was that comment ironic? All he had said was straight out of the basic manual. Perhaps he had misjudged the acting Head of Housing Department; perhaps the younger man was merely indulging the older, perhaps ... but he was right about the hour; they should be back at work in five minutes.

Vladimír leant back against his office door, ran his hands through his tousled hair, sighed deeply and wished it was time to be finishing work, not starting again. The room was empty though clearly Tereza had returned before him; her handbag was on her desk and she had used her lunch break well – there was a shopping bag on the floor.

Suddenly, Vladimír walked over to Tereza's desk. Open to his view on the top of the shopping was an item of children's clothing. Before he had time to think or move, he heard the door behind him open and Tereza walked in.

"Ah, ha!" spluttered Vladimír, acutely aware that he had been caught in the act. "I ... er ... " and he flapped an ineffectual hand towards the shopping bag. Finally, he heard himself lamely observe, "You've been shopping, I see."

Tereza, whose expression had not changed while she deliberately enjoyed Vladimír's embarrassment, walked over and lifted the bag onto the desk. "You are unaware, I take it, that I have a daughter."

Marie, aged about 8 years.

Vladimír backed away. "No, ... er ... I ... No, I had no idea."

"She will be eight years old next week and these ..." Tereza lifted out a patterned summer skirt and blouse "... are for her birthday. There was no need to be embarrassed; I probably ought to have told you before."

"No, no. I have no right to pry into your private life." apologised Vladimír, trying to mend fences, then making it worse by adding, "It's just that you've told me nothing about yourself ..."

"And you are curious!" Tereza smiled, and replaced the clothing in the shopping bag. "I am a very private person, you see. I do not talk about myself, as you will have noticed." She moved round behind her table, and took a deep breath. "But you are right, there are some things you should know."

"No, no, that's fine ..." Vladimír tried to assure her. He sank his hands deep into his trouser pockets and tried to appear nonchalant. "I don't need to know."

"I think you should. I married an Air Force Officer in December 1948, and we moved into a maisonette in the south of the city. It was on the third floor of a large block of flats and overlooked a football stadium."

Tereza wandered over to the observation window, but what she saw was not the interview room, but the first home of her new life.

"There was a large room in which my husband had a desk, and on the wall above he hung an old aeroplane propellor with two blades. They were of wood and highly polished. He told me all about it ... but I have forgotten now. The kitchen and bathroom were both tiny, just room for one to work or wash, but in the main room there was a big sofa ..."

She smiled at the memory, "but unfortunately the whole place was damp."

She turned and stood, head down, with her hands clasped over the child's clothing on the top of her bag. There was a long pause. Vladimír perched on the edge of his desk, facing her, waiting.

"I lost him in an accident just four months after we were married. He had gone through so much, but he had survived, and then we had everything to look forward to. A home ... a family ... friends ... happiness."

Another long pause.

"It was an accident. Something went wrong in the aircraft they told me."

Vlaimir had a sudden longing to take her in his arms and comfort her, but he had the sense to stay quite still, sitting on the edge of his desk.

"Marie was born six months later. And she will be eight next week." Tereza looked up at Vladimír and smiled. That was enough

"Well, what have we to deal with this afternoon?"

"Thank you for telling me," he said simply. "I had no idea. You come and go, and I didn't give you a life outside the office. I was just told your name, and when you would start work ..."

"I ought to tell you also that I have just moved," Tereza added. "Now I have an income I can afford a more healthy flat, and so I live in Bubeneč. You had better have the full address for your file; now I will write it down for you."

It was a thoughtful Vladimír who caught the tram home that evening. He was confused about ideologies, and Janáček's first lecture about the way in which the interests of the individual should be subordinated to the needs of the community. He couldn't fit Tereza into the theory at all.

Had Vladimír been walking in the park one lunchtime some weeks later, he would have seen Tereza sitting on a bench talking with a young woman. If his visual memory had been good he would have recognised the young woman as the one whom he had seen being interviewed by Tereza that morning after he had been teased by Novák and had thrown him unceremoniously out of his office.

The block of flats at Bubeneč.

It was unusual for Council officials to meet members of the public out of office hours. Normally such contacts were to be avoided unless there was a cash bonus in the offing; a condition that certainly did not apply to the meeting between Tereza and Maruška. There was something about the young lady that touched Tereza when she had come that morning to plead for a Council flat – any flat, anywhere, any condition. All the details had been supplied on the appropriate Form but it was the answer to the question, 'Why do you wish to apply for accommodation?' that had caught her attention. There was just the single word, 'Safety', and of course Tereza had probed at the interview but the woman was unwilling to talk.

Now, sitting on a park bench in the open air rather than the claustrophobic, intimidating surroundings of City Hall, Maruška took a chance and broke.

"You see, soon after they came to power, the Communists took over my father's business. Instead of working for himself, he had to work for the Party and sell all his goods to them at ridiculously low prices."

"What was his business?"

"Oh, he had a leather works. Small stuff mainly, gloves, belts, handbags, that sort of thing. But after the war he had expanded and it was just when he was trying to break into the leather boots market that they came."

"Do you know why they did this?"

Maruška took a deep breath. "Yes," she said, and looking intently at Tereza, she revealed quietly, "we were on the wrong side. We were not a Labour family."

Tereza smiled gently. "Go on," she encouraged.

"My father inherited the business from his father who began it back in the Thirties. That put us in the wrong for a start. Then he employed some five or six men, most of whom were unfit for military service and grateful for a living. That was also wrong; they said it was exploitation." She whispered the last word, venomously.

"So what happened?"

"My father was told to release his men and do the work himself; supply the State with ordered goods and if he conducted himself satisfactorily, then in time he might be considered for Party membership."

Tears welled up in her eyes. "My father worked all the hours there were. We helped but he did the heavy stuff. You see, there was just my mother and myself, and to begin with I was still at school. He would not let me leave until I had finished my exams."

Maruška wept quietly. Then she said, "He died last year after his third stroke. My mother is so frightened. They have closed the business and want us to leave. That is why I need a flat – where my mother will be safe and not dread every day being thrown out of our house onto the street."

So began a friendship. They started to meet regularly; at first in the park, later in out-of-the-way cafes and bars. Sometimes they shared an evening meal, and Marie would join them. Maruška saw Marie as a much younger version of herself. She had grown up in the heyday of the Revolution; had enjoyed the local sports Club, had been canoeing at summer camps and ski-ing in the mountains in the winter. She knew no different – until her father's business was taken over and through the eyes of sympathisers, saw disillusion set in among those who had been genuine believers.

It was at one of these meetings that Tereza revealed a secret that only Marie knew, though she was unaware of its significance. Tereza said that her husband, before the Revolution, had been in England. There he had made a friend of a British Air Force officer and they had corresponded when Stanislav returned to Prague. Then she said that she – Tereza –, still wrote to this man and he responded. To have a friend in the West was something you kept very much to yourself; they were capitalists, and if you wanted to know how to treat them you had only to look at Berlin.

Maruška noticed, as Tereza had done earlier, that the divisions of a capitalist society were appearing in Communist ranks. Those who drove new cars and wore new, fashionable clothes were all Party Members. If a good post became vacant, you approached the local Party Secretariat; who you knew was more important than your talent, and if you had access to foreign currency and were of a generous disposition, the post was yours.

The friendship flourished. In time, Tereza was able to make a maisonette available for Maruška and her mother; not the best but it provided the safety and mental comfort they needed while Maruška completed her training as a nurse.

Marie grew in stature and maturity: she was a bright girl and did well at school.

So the Fifties became the Sixties, and a man named Dubček rose to the top of the Party ranks.

Born in 1921, Alexander Dubček's rise to become leader of the Communist Party in Czechoslovakia was unremarkable. It was only in his later years that a dedicated Party member might have raised a frown at some of his pronouncements and policies. It was not easy for him to convince the hardliners in his Government that the war against capitalism would be the more effectively waged were the Communist isolation policy to be modified.

Thus the early months of 1968 became known as the 'Springtime of Freedom'. Gradually real news began to appear in Czechoslovak newspapers, on television and radio. To beat your enemy, you have to know him; his weapons, his policies and above all, his thinking. Thus Dubček persuaded his colleagues to permit the limited import of foreign literature. Only in this way would the people realise the decadence of the West.

Perhaps he did believe this; perhaps he took the view that a foot in both camps was the wisest policy for a relatively poor mid-European country. In the event, a spirit of freedom began to pervade Czechoslovakia – to the dismay of other Warsaw Pact countries. Criticism of the regime began to appear in the Press – the exposure of corruption in high places; anger expressed at housing conditions and frustration at beaurocratic oppression. There were letters of warning, indeed of protest from the Party leaders in East Germany, in Poland and Hungary which did little to deter Dubček and his increasing band of followers.

It may have been this change of climate which brought about a momentous decision for Tereza and Marie. It was the autumn of 1966 when a letter from England arrived at their flat in Bubeneč. Tereza slit it open and read in silence. Then she shouted, "Marie, Marie, your father's friend, Charles, is inviting you to visit them in England! Look, let us translate it together."

So they sat side by side and excitedly worked out, sentence by sentence, just what Charles had written. Would Marie like to come to spend the summer holiday with them and their children? To arrive in late July and return at the end of August? They would visit the south west of the country and stay in a cottage by the sea. "The sea!" exclaimed Marie excitedly, "Oh, Mami, the sea!" She had seen lakes, but only pictures of the water stretching away to the horizon.

"We must think about this carefully, Marie. There are two questions. First, do you want to go – to a strange country among people you do not know, where there will be no one to whom you can turn when you cannot understand?"

"Yes, yes, Mami. I realise that, but you have told me my father liked England and the people there, so that's good enough for me."

"Now, Marie, stop and think ..."

"Yes, Mami. I want to go!"

"Oh, you are so impatient! Very well then, let us look ahead. The second question is whether the authorities will allow your visit. If you wanted to see other socialist countries it would be easier, but permission to fly to London and stay with English people might be refused."

"I will ask then."

Tereza smiled at her daughter's spirit. "You may be as tall as me, but in law you are still a child so I will have to apply for you. Now off you go, and Marie ... we will resume our English lessons, this week."

"Yes, Mami."

"And Marie ..."

"Yes, Mami?"

"You do not mention this holiday to anyone; not your best friends, nor your teachers, nor the bus driver, nor ..."

"But, Mami ..."

"No, Marie, no!"

How difficult it had been over the years, striking the balance. Remembering always to remind Marie to wear her red headscarf ; parrying questions ("I like Maruška – why has her family had such a rough time?); making sure she attended Young Communist camps; teaching her English, a language which Marie could practise only on the very few English visitors she might meet. Above all, how to present her father, that confident, courageous man (– there were so many of his qualities in his daughter –) who fought for his country with men who were now to be viewed as virtual enemies; whom she had loved and about whom she judged to say so little to his daughter.

Tereza obtained the standard Form of Application for Travel outside Czechoslovakia and completed it on behalf of her daughter. Only one question caused serious thought - 'Purpose of Visit?' She drafted several responses before finally settling on, 'To be a good ambassador for her country and its people.' She then added that the Principal of her school would act as a character referee.

This was a shrewd move on Tereza's part. In the first place all such Principals were political appointments and thus his word would be accepted by the authorities, and secondly Marie had just graduated with some distinction and been awarded one of the few available places at the prestigious Art College – the Grafická Škola – in Prague. She was riding high as one of the school's successful students.

It took several months for a decision to be reached. Finally, permission was granted for Marie to visit England for a limit of four weeks only; that she was to travel unaccompanied, and that she was to report on her return to her local Party office.

These conditions were clearly designed to discourage her from making the journey; if anything they made her more determined than ever to visit the country and the people with whom her mysterious father had found the comradeship which a common military cause engenders.

In the last week of July, Tereza waved to Marie in her lovely red coat as she boarded a flight to London Heathrow from Ruzyně airport just outside Prague. It was to be her first flight and her first visit outside the country.

Marie wrote from England about her flight; about her welcome, about the family who treated her like one of their own. She wrote about some of the unusual customs in England; about the places she had seen and the people she met. And the sea! And the family holiday by the sea in an area of England called Devon where they joined another family of friends – all one big party. And – as Teresa noticed – how her English was improving … and then how she was looking forward to returning to Prague and speaking Czech language again.

In the two years that followed, Marie completed her Course at the elite Grafická Škola and took her Final examinations. She spent her summer holiday picking hops and thought of her young friends in England enjoying themselves beside the sea. For them it really was a holiday; for her it was another kind of work. And in 1968, she again applied for and was granted leave to re-visit England after her examinations were complete. On this second occasion, it was a much more mature young lady who boarded the flight at Ruzyně airport. This was largely a matter of natural development but as she and Tereza were aware, accelerated by the flood of Western publications and radio broadcasts. Dubček's liberal policies had ensured that those with ears and eyes knew much more about the world outside the Socialist countries.

The matter of Dubček's reforms concerned the Socialist block. There was an increasingly virulent campaign in the Soviet Press, while talks between officials of the Czechoslovak Government and Soviet leaders gave the outside world the impression that all was well, they did nothing to deter Dubček and his followers from their chosen course.

In the last week of July, Marie flew again to England leaving an increasing tension between the Warsaw Pact countries and the government in Prague. There were reports in the British media of an ominous build-up of troops along the Polish and Soviet borders.

At the family home in England, Charles noted these developments with apprehension but kept his thoughts to himself; he did not want to spoil the holiday which was going splendidly – everyone picking up where they had left off two years previously.

On the morning of 21st August, sixty thousand troops of the USSR, East Germany, Poland, Hungary and Bulgaria invaded Czechoslovakia. The radio warned people not on vital public work to remain calm and indoors but this was largely ignored. Emil Zátopec, the Czechoslovak Olympic Gold Medallist, appeared in Wenceslas Square in his full Colonel's uniform, mounted a monument and harangued the crowd: there was even sporadic resistance as barriers and obstructions were hastily constructed. But all to no avail: Tereza watched as troops in armoured cars and transporters poured through the suburb of Bubeneč towards the City centre. She left the radio on and heard the last message broadcast before the Russians stormed the transmitter: *"Don't forget us! Remember us, even when our resistance has finished, and the rest of the world has found other things to think about."*

Tereza spent that evening at her cousin, Šíma's, flat. It was company, but in keeping with the solemnity of events they both sat much of the time in companionable silence.

Suddenly, the telephone rang. It startled Tereza – unused to a phone in her flat – that sudden summons out of the silence as if it had no right to disturb the vacuum that the room and indeed Prague itself, that dark and frightened city, had become.

Šíma stared at the phone for several seconds, and then moved across the room and picked it up.

"Yes," she said. There was a pause while she listened intently and then wordlessly handed the phone to Teresa.

"Mami, Mami, are you safe?" Marie's voice was as clear as if she were in the next room.

When she put the phone down Tereza dissolved into tears. It was to be four long years before she saw her daughter again.

VI

Marie, and Family

August 1968. ENGLAND.

"Your Mother may well understand after twenty years under Soviet Communism, but I do think – before you make up your mind to stay here – that you should telephone your Mother and let her know what you propose!"

Charles tried to conceal with gentle words his utter astonishment at Marie's announcement. The family had not moved. "Danny, fetch the phone book and let's find out the international code for Czechoslovakia. Emma, pencil and paper, please."

The spell broken, the family gathered round and worked out the complete number to dial. "It will not work. They will have the lines broken," prophesied Marie rather defiantly. "And in any case, my Mother has no phone."

"Well, how can you get in touch with her? You must have made some arrangement before you left Prague."

"My Mother's cousin, Šíma, works for the phone Company so she is able to have a phone in her flat. Perhaps she would arrange a time when my Mother could visit her."

"Good idea – go and try to arrange something. Now." requested Charles, a shade more firmly.

Marie swept up the paper and departed to the hall where the phone was located. They heard her settle into the adjacent chair. "Shut the door," said Mary quietly.

"Oh, can't we listen?" asked Emma.

"No, you know that's very bad manners," replied Mary.

"And in any case," added Charles, "your knowledge of the Czech language is not up to rapid-fire pace yet. If she gets through she'll be talking to her Mother in her mother-tongue and none of us would understand one word. But there's something more important. Now just sit down and concentrate, both of you. It may be; just may be, that Marie could be marooned in this country – for how long we have no idea. How do you feel about her becoming one of us, about living with us? Not just for a holiday but indefinitely." He paused.

"It will mean sharing; not just two of you but between three of you. And she will be the eldest, remember, and probably have different interests from you ..."

A pause, and quite clearly they could hear Marie's raised voice despite the closed door.

"Good Lord, she has got through!" exclaimed Charles, "never thought she would."

"No, nor did I," added Mary, and then turning back to the children, "Think about what your Dad has just said. It's very important. Turn it round: suppose you had been on holiday in Prague and for some reason you couldn't get back here. You'd be terribly homesick for a start and then ..."

The door opened suddenly and Marie said, "Charles, my Mother is with Šíma now. Please come and speak to her."

He heaved himself out of his chair and followed Marie into the hall. They heard him say, "Hello," and there was more in English before Marie intervened and acted as translator.

"We can't let her go back," said Danny, "not to face that lot!" and he nodded towards the television screen where they had all seen the military occupation of Prague only a few hours before. "Yes," agreed Emma, "I'm all for her staying with us." Then she turned to her Mother and asked thoughtfully, "If Marie stays with us, do we have to call Daddy 'Charles'?"

When they returned, Charles announced, "Well, we have another member of the family – at least for the time being." And they hugged Marie, and Marie hugged them back and burst into tears.

"Now," said Mary, being her practical self again, "Marie had started to pack her things. Emma, go upstairs and help her to unpack. And we want her room to be a little bit of Prague for her, so find out what she would like in there. Pictures and things. Let's see what we can do to make her feel at home. Danny, clear up outside. Bikes away in the shed; all tidy now. Charles dear, help me with supper."

And it was all busy-ness. Kitchen door shut, Mary leant against the dresser. "Well?"

"Very difficult speaking through a translator – handing the phone backwards and forwards. And no choice really. Tereza said – if Marie was accurate – that she was not to return at the present time, it was too dangerous. To wait and see what happens by Christmas. And then she asked me to take good care of Marie ... of course, I gave my word."

"Yes, you had to. Of all the possibilities we could foresee before we invited her here, this was not one. If you had told me twenty four hours ago that we would have another daughter, I would have put you down for the funny farm." A pause, and then she added with a wry smile, "At least her arrival was easier than the other two!"

"Supper ready?" asked Danny, bursting in through the back door.

In bed that night, Charles and Mary laid immediate plans. "First thing in the morning is to phone the Czechoslovak Embassy. Let's see what they have to say."

"What happens when our two ..."

"Don't say that any more; it's our *three*."

"Alright! What happens when our two younger ones ... go back to school? Does she go with them? Or to the local College? Or do we try to get her a job?"

"Well, not the school I would have thought."

"Yes. I mean I think you're right there. God, it's hot: do you really want the cover on?"

A pause.

"Charles, do we have to adopt her ... legally, I mean?"

Slowly he turned over to face Mary. "Do you know," he replied slowly, "I haven't the faintest idea."

"Well, I reckon it's important. I mean ... she's in limbo now. She's a Czechoslovak citizen ... where does she stand as far as our laws are concerned? Is she an immigrant? What's more important, where do we stand?"

"She may still be technically a child in Prague; in fact, I would have thought more than likely. When is she nineteen?"

"Next birthday."

"Yes, I know that, but when is it?"

"September, ... next month. Have to look the date up; it's in my diary."

"Right. Second phone call of the morning is to our solicitor. Not that he's likely to know either. 'I'll take advice,' he'll say."

Charles yawned and kissed his wife goodnight, a ritual he never broke. But neither could find sleep. At something past one, Mary slipped downstairs and made a pot of tea.

Charles smiled, sipped the hot drink and wished his dear wife had brought the whisky bottle instead.

Mary leant back on the pillows, smiled sweetly at her dear husband and asked, "Have you worked out how much weekly pocket money you are allowing Marie? Presuming you will operate a sliding scale in relation to the present recipients, and you will of course be aware that at eighteen a girl does need a dress allowance."

"I take it that you have already worked out the regular basis on which we are to consume Czechoslovak food. The recipes for dumplings, pickled cabbage and so forth are buzzing round in your head, and you are about to ask me to lay in a sizeable quantity of Czech beer."

Charles dumped his tea mug on the nearby table, thumped the pillow and turned his back on his wife. Mary switched off the light, and pinched her husband's bottom – hard.

The following morning, Charles was up early and off to his office where he shut the door and switched his phone to an outside line. Shortly after, he phoned Mary at home.

"Is Marie up yet?"

"You must be joking! No, fast asleep still."

"Well, rouse her; rinse, dry and package her at the front door. I'm picking her up in ten minutes."

"Alladin will find the magic lamp. Any particular reason?"

"We're off to London. I've talked to some chap at the Czech Embassy; very helpful, anything we want in documentation – Work Permits, that sort of thing – but he says to get there before they're taken over, so it's a smartish take-off. Oh, and make sure Marie has her Passport with her"

"Right. Anything else?"

"Flask of coffee would be acceptable."

"You'll be lucky!"

They made it in time. The Embassy officials were helpful and thrust a wad of leaflets, permits and application forms at them. Nor were they the only people there; Charles was surprised by a queue, mostly of young men and women all, apparently, in similar circumstances. Marie clearly enjoyed animated though often solemn conversations and Charles experienced an unexpected sense of frustration at his inability to understand what other people were saying. 'I suppose that's what Marie must have been feeling to some extent this last month," he admitted to himself. He looked at the faces of the young people there. How many, he wondered, have a family to look after them? How many are on their own having perhaps taken seasonal employment to earn more than they would in their own country, and now taken the same decision as Marie, but in precarious circumstances?

Despite the heat of August in Central Europe, Prague was a cold city again. Tereza felt the pervasive atmosphere of watching one's step, thinking about every word before saying as little as possible; hear nothing, see nothing, say nothing all over again. All the relaxations that the Dubček regime had fostered were abruptly halted.

Dubček himself disappeared – presumably for rehabilitation – and the government passed into the hands of those whom the Warsaw Pact countries could trust, … under supervision, of course. The country found itself back under the strict confines of a Communist society, and the life and gaiety that had recently re-established itself in the restaurants and clubs, on the pavements and the parks, evaporated like the morning mists that hung over the Vltava river when the sun warmed the old city.

Tereza answered the quiet knock at her door and let in Maruška. They had abandoned meeting in public now and enjoyed each other's home hospitality.

Tereza made coffee, served the lovely sweet pastries and cakes that she had bought that morning from the nearby patisserie and settled down to talk.

"How is your mother?"

"She is as well as she is ever likely to be," conceded Maruška. "She does not want to go out much now. She sits and reads, and looks at old photographs and tells me stories about her family that I have heard so many times before."

"Yes, the troops about the city will have brought back the unhappiest of memories for her."

"It's no use trying to jolly her along; to get her to go out. She has very few friends left now and has just withdrawn into herself. But that's my problem; let's be more cheerful. Did Marie enjoy her holiday in England? Where is she this evening?"

It was Tereza's turn.

A deep intake of breath. "That is my problem. Well, no; it's more a problem solved for her. She is still in England."

"Still in England! But that's incredible ..."

"No. You see, Marie was due to fly back in the evening of the 21st, that was Thursday of last week. And as you know, they marched in at dawn on the Wednesday so she had not left her hosts. She saw what happened here on television news broadcasts over there and later that night she phoned me. She said ... she wanted to stay with her friends in England."

Maruška moved across and knelt in front of Tereza, holding her hands.

"Oh, my dear Tereza!" Instinctively, she knew how the older woman was torn apart and that no words could begin to compensate for the loss – however temporary – of her only daughter.

"I shall, of course, write to her but I think it wise to send the letters to my sister who lives near Brno. She can arrange for them to be posted over the border in Austria."

"Do you think it is that serious?" asked Maruška.

"I do not know but it is important that I don't prejudice either my own position nor that of Marie when she wishes to return."

"Has she written to you?"

"Of course, but that was before the troops moved in. It may be some time before the next letter."

"Do you think she will telephone again?"

"No. She was lucky in that they had not taken over the telegraph system by Wednesday evening. I have already written telling her not to try."

Maruška knelt silently, surprised that Tereza seemed almost to be trying to cut herself off from Marie. But she knew it was for Marie's own good – hurting Tereza more that it might hurt her daughter.

"I kept the radio on all day," said Tereza very quietly. "I heard the last message before it went off, – about remembering us. I hope it was heard in England and broadcast there: perhaps Marie would hear it."

She leant forward and gently stroked Maruška's hair. "She is in good hands. I spoke to the man whom my husband knew; he said he would look after her. Yes, I shall write; I shall not let them forget us. Now do get up! You must be very stiff kneeling there. I will go and make fresh coffee."

Marie, summer 1969.

By mid-September, Danny and Emma were back at school and among their own friends again. Mary knew that would happen; but what to do about Marie? The enormity of what she had done finally dawned and it became essential to find something to engage her energies. Such Courses as were available at the local College did not take her printing skills forward and there was nothing else on offer which took her interest.

"We must find her a job," opined Charles.

"Your talent for stating the obvious has never been clearer," was Mary's withering response. "What job? Where? Please be helpful. There is nothing in the printing field; I've been to see Stephen and he says he's over-staffed at the local paper. If she's going to continue in that field then she has to move away, and she's not ready to do that yet. It's got to be something else just as a stop-gap. Or she has to change career."

"Problems, problems ... yes, I agree with your diagnosis. We'll have to think of something." And he did the very next day, or to be more accurate, a temporary solution presented itself.

After the evening meal, the family were sitting round the kitchen table – that is except for Charles who had not arrived. Marie had picked up one of Danny's science exercise books and was studying the cover. "What is this?" she asked. "Einstein I know, but what does this mean?"

Scrawled across the cover were the words, 'Einstein Rules Relatively, OK?' and then underneath in a different hand, 'well, in theory anyway."

"Well," said Danny, scratching his ear, "it's a play on words. You know that Einstein worked out a theory of Relativity – don't ask me about that 'cos I don't understand a word of it – but we know he did, and that's tied in with the idea that so-and-so rules if he's top dog and no one can understand Einstein so he must be top dog because no one can disprove him, and so he must rule. OK?"

"Danny, that's cruel! Marie didn't get a word of that."

"Didn't get a word of what?" asked Charles opening the door.

"Late again," came the chorus.

"Late I may be, but I come bringing news. Opportunity would be a better word. I've been talking with John down at the packing station and he's desperate for temporary labour. Marie, how do you feel about spending some days packing vegetables and fruit – and getting paid for it?"

"I do not know this. What is it I must do?"

Of course, everyone spoke at the same time about the large brick building on the edge of the town where all the local produce came to be sorted, cleaned and packed appropriately for distribution, not only in the district but as far afield as Covent Garden Market, the lorries rolling out of town from the early hours of the morning onwards. Charles and Mary held their planning session, as usual, after bedroom doors were shut for the night.

"I'll take her down to see John in the morning and I'm sure he'll show her round. Then she can observe the working men and women of England."

"Yes," said Charles, "It's time she saw and got to know some other people. More importantly, it will be the first step towards independence for her. What line do you think John is likely to put her on?"

"I should think the egg-packing. It's the cleanest job – if any can be described as clean – and probably the quietest. Or put another way, the area where she will pick up fewer of the offensive words in the English language!"

So it was that Marie experienced her first working day, sorting, grading and packing eggs. The hours dragged slowly by; she understood only a proportion of the girls' gossip that went on incessantly around her; appeared indifferent to the whistles and shout of the lads (though probably quite pleased) but was delighted by her first pay packet. She showed everyone and counted the contents afresh each time.

If Charles and Mary had expected her to acquire an extended vocabulary from her new environment they were not disappointed – but it came from an entirely unexpected quarter.

Maruška in national costume, happy and cheerful, but the military man on her shoulder does not seem to be enjoying his day.

"Why do English people always talk the weather? If it is raining; if the sun shines – always they talk about it! Why is it so interesting?"

"Do we do that?" asked Charles.

"Of course we do," rejoined Mary.

"This morning," continued Marie, "was normal day. Tracey said was lovely day, and big girl with hair scarf said was wonderful, and when George come he said was nice and hot. Have they not seen sun before?"

"Yes. That sort of conversation does happen. You see, the weather in England is so variable – never the same two days running – that it's worth a comment." Charles' explanation did not satisfy Marie.

"In Prague, we talk important things. Who's having baby; what to eat for dinner. Weather does not matter."

Mary came up with the practical advice. "In future, Marie, just agree with anyone about the weather. If we've had a storm all night and they say it's a nice day, you say 'Yes, it's lovely, isn't it', and they'll all think you're English!"

"And if you don't like doing that, just start with 'Good morning' – that's quite safe."

Danny looked up from his homework. "Dad, did you know that 'Good Morning' doesn't mean 'Have a good morning'. Our English teacher says it's a contraction from a greeting centuries old which meant 'God guide you this morning'. Just the same as 'Goodbye' is a contraction of 'God be with you'."

"More play with words!" Marie was not impressed.

"Not really," said Danny, "but I've got a good one for you here. What about 'Vampires are a pain in the neck!'? You see, we have a phrase in English ... "

Charles shut the door on what promised to become a complicated conversation.

Later that night, Charles confided to Mary, "I know Danny takes O–levels this year but I reckon he's set his sights on coaching Marie through the English Language exam. You know, today's lesson in school becomes this evening's educating-Marie session."

"At least it means Danny's going over the lesson again. That's something."

"Yes, and there's something else. I know Tereza mentioned reviewing the situation at Christmas but I can't see it. Life's no easier for people in Prague. Do you think Marie ought to fill in that application for British nationality?"

Tereza took the phone call from Maruška at work. She would not be able to visit her that night as her mother had been taken into hospital and she would be spending the evening with her. Finally Tereza said she would meet Maruška at the hospital: a time was agreed, and they went to a nearby café.

"So. How is your mother this evening?"

"Oh, I do not know; there seems nothing physically wrong with her. They took her in because she is losing weight; I can't get her to eat anything substantial."

"They will do their best for her. As you are one of the nurses there, your mother will not lack treatment or attention."

"Oh, I know ... but it's so ... worrying."

"Come now. I know it's getting late, but let's order coffee. I have had another letter from Marie through my sister near Brno. – Here! Two Vienna Coffee, please, – and she is so amusing."

Maruška wondered. She was well aware just how much Tereza was missing her daughter – was this a show of bravado?

"What does she say that you find amusing then?"

"You know the reputation the English have for being pet-lovers. Well, Marie says that they also have other unusual habits: for example, you know how we use forks at table. Like other people on this continent, we take the fork in our right hand and scoop up the food – Marie says we use it like a shovel. In England she says they have the knife in their right hand and the fork in their left, and use it *upside down!* Yes, they push their food onto it and hope it is still there when the fork reaches the mouth."

"What? Not peas, surely!"

"Of course! Some of the food falls off and onto the floor ... which is why so many English people keep a dog. It's to clear up spilt food!"

They both laughed and sipped their coffee.

"I have also had a letter from my late husband's friend, Charles. He tells me that Marie is well; that she is trying hard to fit into an English family, and that she is working – temporarily – packing eggs into containers."

"How many has she dropped?"

"Ah, he does not tell me ... but I am happy that she is safe."

Maruška thought about that last remark, long after they had parted for the night.

Christmas came and went. The family made sure Marie had lots of presents, and the large parcel which had arrived from Tereza some days before was secreted so that she could have it on Christmas Day morning. Seeing the postmark, Marie tore it open and shouted with delight as some of her winter skirts and jumpers spilled out. "What a marvellous present even though they are your own clothes!" enthused Mary. "They will make you think of home." and Marie grabbed a skirt and jumper and rushed upstairs to put them on. While she was out of the room, Mary took the other garments and shook them out. Suddenly she stopped and felt along the hem of a skirt. "There's something hidden in here," she said. With Marie's agreement, she cut through an inch or two of the stitching while the family gathered round. This was the stuff of detective novels and none of them wanted to miss the revelation. Mary prised out a small piece of coarse cloth which, when unwrapped, contained a gold ring. "Oh!" exclaimed Marie, "Look, my Mother gave this to me on sixteen birthday! Oh,

I am glad to have it again." She slipped the ring on, and laughed and kissed Mary, and then because it was Christmas, went round the room and kissed everyone else. Danny blushed.

Emma persuaded Marie to accompany them to Church, but singing was not Marie's strong point – not even tuneful Carols.

New Year came and went. The routines of work and school had no sooner started than there were further horrific television pictures from Prague

On the 19th January 1969, a 19 year-old student, Jan Palach, walked into Wenceslas Square, doused himself thoroughly in petrol and set himself alight. He was barely alive when he eventually reached hospital. A furious crowd gathered and expressed their anger by obliterating the newly-painted signs which read 'Red Army Square' and replaced them with 'Jan Palach Square'. The young man died from his burns two days later. This very public protest against the iron regime imposed by Kuzněto v from the Soviet Politburo who had replaced Dubček and now gave the orders, was beamed around the world.

"You were quite right not to go back," said Mary putting a comforting arm around Marie, but to Charles later she confided, "How do you comfort someone who's just seen those pictures, who's stood just where that young man stood, and who can feel so much more than we can because it's her home?"

Spring gave way to Summer. Danny, caught between Charles and the school, gave in and started to work seriously for his exams. Emma, no longer a 'new girl', became rather fashion-conscious and blasé.

Marie continued to pack eggs. Sometimes when there was a rush order or surplus crop, she moved to fruit or vegetable lines, but eventually she found herself back on eggs. It was agreed by everybody that eggs would never be served for breakfast.

Then, in late summer, just a year after she had arrived, a suitable vacancy arose at a printing works in a neighbouring town. Charles telephoned and spoke to the Manager of the design department. Would they, he asked, be prepared to consider for the advertised vacancy a Czechoslovak girl who had studied at the Grafická Škola in Prague. There was a moment's pause, then, "Yes, indeed. I would like to see her very soon – with examples of her work."

"I'm afraid examples of her work won't be possible. You see ... " and after fifteen minutes of explanation, an interview had been arranged.

Marie was questioned closely by the manager and other members of his team. Over an hour later, he emerged to tell Charles and Mary that they were impressed and had offered Marie the post. He was sorry for the delay but "Can't afford to make a mistake, you know."

So having said her Goodbyes to the friendly folk at the Packing Station, Marie began the kind of work for which she had been trained. She caught a bus at an unearthly hour of the morning, and Mary put the evening meal back half an hour to accommodate her return. In the next letter to her Mother, Marie wrote about another English peculiarity. "You know that in Prague, the bus will always pull up at bus-stops unless the conductor has rung the bell in which case he drives on. Here it's the other way round: you ring the bell if you want the bus to stop. Crazy people! Buses that don't stop at Bus-stops unless you tell them to! What's the point of having Bus-stops?"

She would not have asked Danny that question, but she did ask the family at large, "What is Esso Tiger?"

"It's a petrol advertisement," replied Charles. 'Put a Tiger in your tank!' is the slogan. Keep your eyes open when you go past garages; you'll see the advert."

"Why do you ask?" Emma wondered.

"Because big notice in our office says 'Remember Esso Tiger was born here!'"

"Gosh, was it really?"

"I didn't know that," said Charles. "Must be a high-powered firm. You did well to get a place there, Marie. Should make you feel superior!"

"What is 'superior'?" Marie asked Danny, but he was busy writing on the cover of an exercise book, 'Feel Superior – Become a Nun.'

Tereza and Maruška continued to meet and became closer after Maruška's mother died. Tereza still worked in the Housing Department at City Hall where Vladimír had been given another assistant – this time the kind of pretty youngster for which he had hoped when Tereza was appointed. However hard he tried though, Otti had his measure and while perfectly friendly, kept him at arm's length. Tereza was tempted to feel quite sorry for poor Vladimír.

"He has even smartened himself up; bought new shirts and ties, and keeps a comb in a drawer," she confided to Maruška, "not that he can always remember which drawer he has put it in!"

"Has Otti no time for him at all then?"

"Not in the way he would wish," Tereza continued. "He brings her little presents which she accepts gracefully enough, but if he gets too close she always finds an excuse to slip out of his way. She thinks he's old, you see."

"There must be, what ... ten years between them?"

"At least. But he's more considerate since she's been working there. Do you know, he asked me last week how Marie was, and what was I buying for her birthday this year! She was only eight when he first discovered I had a daughter and it was her birthday. And he remembered, you see."

"Does he know ... know where she is?"

"Heavens! No! I told him that she was well and growing into a fine young lady but just let him think that she was still living with me."

"Yes, that is wise." A pause, then Maruška asked, "Are you sure it is better for her to be in England with strangers, than living with you here ... where she grew up?"

"Yes, I am sure," responded Tereza carefully. "Nothing lasts for ever, not even cruelty and brutality. There will come a time when she can come back, and she will know what it is to have lived in a country where there is freedom of movement, and speech and thought."

Marie seemed to enjoy her new work – at least she was largely familiar with the tasks the design department faced. There was also a social life in which she joined; often a phone call told the family not to wait supper for her – she would be on a later bus.

"I think it's fine," Charles suggested. "She's making new friends and developing her independence."

"That's all very well," rejoined Mary, "but we don't know what sort of company she's keeping or what she gets up to on these social evenings."

"Oh, do stop worrying! If she's bothered she'll come to you for advice or help. She regards you as a mother confessor."

"Well, I hope she comes before she needs help, that's all. We are rather responsible, you know, despite her being twenty next month. Her mother would blame us if anything happened to her."

But the first 'event' in which Marie was involved was quite unexpected. She had been with the printing firm about a year when she arrived home, very late, carrying a large bouquet of flowers and wearing a gaudy sash. Clearly elated, she pirouetted round the room and declaimed, "I am Miss Print!"

The family dissolved into gusts of laughter. It was, of course, Danny who suggested that she should make a slight pause between pronouncing 'Miss' and 'Print', otherwise she was liable to misinterpretation! Then came her explanation. All the personnel at the works voted each year for their Beauty Queen, and at an evening Dinner, the winner was announced. This year she had been chosen; had had to go up and receive her Sash, be congratulated and kissed on both cheeks by the Managing Director, and receive the cheers and whistles of the assembled company.

Charles broke out a bottle and the family celebrated in style. Marie had achieved her first distinction in her adopted land: if there had been an emptiness, if there had been a feeling of being on the outside, then this went a long way to developing a sense of belonging at last.

The following Sunday afternoon, Mary and Charles took the dog for a long walk. They were glad to get out of the house for lunch had finished with a somewhat tense atmosphere. Marie had casually asked Danny what the word 'monger' meant.

Danny, now well into his A.level course, and self-appointed guardian of the English Language from Czechoslovak unorthodoxy, promptly stated that there was no such word.

But Marie persisted. "There is old shop in Church Street being made new."

"Yes, renovated."

"They have painted new front, and word over door is 'Fishmonger'. Fish I know; what is 'monger'?"

"Ah, yes. Well, you can have it joined onto another word, but it isn't a word on its own."

"Must have meaning if joined onto other word. In Slav languages, we have similar. You have 'fingers' and silly word 'toes'. We have joined up word 'foot-fingers'; logical to have fingers on hands and fingers on foots."

"FEET!"

"Don't shout, Danny!" from the end of the table.

"So what does 'mong' mean?" persisted Marie.

"There's no such word, I tell you." hissed Danny.

Emma had slipped out of the room and returned with her large dictionary. "We'll see who's right. Now then – N, back a bit, Me ... Mi ... Mo ... Monday, money, monger. There, it is in. It says, 'a dealer, except in a few instances eg:ironmonger, one who trafficks in a discreditable way. Used to mean a slave-trader'. There now." She passed the open book to Danny, and added with a smirk, "Apologies expected ..."

Good humour might have returned to the table had not Marie, who rarely got the better of an argument over words, decided to rub it in. To Emma, she muttered about a crazy language ... then held up one finger. "Finger." She held up two, "You tell me to add letter 's' to make 'fingers'. Fine." Then she pointed down below the table.

"At end of leg, I have foot. At end of other leg, I have foot. I have two legs, but not two foots. Will Academy Danny please tell me why I don't have foots?"

"Good fresh air," breathed Charles as they swung down the lane towards the fifty acre.

"Going back to Wednesday evening," said Mary, "when Marie came in as Miss Print. Notice anything ... unusual?"

"Apart from having 'Employee of the Year' making Whoopee round the kitchen table – no. Just what part of that celebration are you referring to?"

"Notice what time she came in? No, well, doesn't matter, but there's no bus at that time. Yesterday I asked her how she got back and she told me Julian had brought her home in his car. Apparently he doesn't work at the printers; someone took her to a meeting of the local Young Farmers' Club and she met him there."

"Bound to happen sooner or later. She's attractive and personable, and it's natural for some fellow to suggest a lift might be more congenial than the late bus."

"Yes," said Mary thoughtfully. "Remember the sorts of things that happened when you took me home in your car? I told her that if Julian gave her a lift home again, then she was to bring him in; you would want to see him."

"Thank you very much! I'll bet that put her off."

"On the contrary! She said she'd like us to meet him."

They walked on in silence for a few moments.

"Look at that stupid dog! Even he's trying to chase the birds now. Come here! Oh, into the stream after a moorhen ... No! Don't shake yourself all over me!"

By the end of 1972, Prague had settled back into the old ways of Communist life. Odd outbursts of cries for freedom were ruthlessly suppressed. Alexander Dubček had disappeared – he was last seen being bundled unceremoniously into the back of an armoured car on the evening of the invasion back in 1968 – though the Soviet Press reported in March 1970 that he had been suspended from the Communist Party, and then in June of that year that he had been expelled from the Party. Some suggested that his 'rehabilitation' had been so unsuccessful that he had been given up as a bad job; other realists thought he had been shot.

For Tereza though, the end of the year brought joy. She could hardly wait for her next meeting with Maruška. "I have news, such news!", she whispered, "Marie is coming to visit ... early in the New Year!"

"What? How is that possible?"

"She is coming as a tourist! Yes, it is complicated as she now has a British passport, but she is registered here as a Czech national legally living abroad. Therefore, she must travel on her Czech passport and she has papers from our Embassy in London permitting her to visit Prague. Oh, and I must tell you she is bringing a young man with her – someone she has met over there. His name is Julian; his family are farmers. They are travelling by road. Isn't it splendid?"

"How wonderful for you! You will arrange for me to see her, won't you?"

"Of course! We can take this young man round our city ... " Suddenly, Tereza became her usual quiet self again. "We will show him what it is like to live in virtual captivity."

"But to see Marie again! What a wonderful Christmas present for you!"

"Yes, indeed. I am so grateful; I wondered if I would ever see her again."

And see her again she did.

VII

Marie and Julian

1972 ENGLAND

Marie was as good as her word.

A few weeks after Mary and Charles had become aware that she was being brought home by an escort, Marie irrupted late one evening into the hall amid gales of laughter followed by a young man of about her own age, perhaps a year or two older. "This is Julian!" Marie announced, introducing him round to the sleepy family. Charles was over six feet, but Julian stood above him by several inches. On the willowy side, he sported a full head of fair hair down to his shoulders. A tweedy jacket, corduroy trousers and heavy boots completed his appearance: no one was left in doubt as to his agricultural connection.

What Mary noticed were his extremely large hands. Round the room he went, grasping other hands in a fierce grip, grinning happily. Finally, he shook hands with Charles.

"Care for a beer?"

"Yes, thanks very much."

Charles departed and returned from the kitchen with two glasses and cans. He poured the first and handed it to Julian. By the time he had poured the second, Julian was half way down his glass and seated next to Mary with whom he was engaged in animated discussion about the price of potatoes.

It was just before midnight that Julian realised he should not overstay his welcome on his first visit to Marie's 'home'.

Thereafter, Julian became a regular visitor though Charles was moved to point out that while he was welcome to stay as long as he liked at weekends, "Some of us have to get up to work on weekdays!"

Then he asked, as an afterthought, "What time do you have to be at work?"

"Oh, I'm usually around the yard by seven," replied Julian, and then added without a trace of malice, "and at weekends, of course."

"You know," confided Charles to Mary, "that young man rather grows on one, I find."

The family was growing up. Danny left school and joined a local Bank. Emma, quite the young lady now, became involved with the real world of public examinations. Marie moved away into a small, self-contained flat from which she could walk to work. She and Julian often turned up sometime over the weekend, and it was on a Saturday family night out at a local restaurant that Julian turned to Marie and asked, "Why don't you visit your Mother? You could, you know, now you have dual nationality."

Simple though the question was, no one else seemed to have thought of it. It dominated the conversation for the rest of the evening and wouldn't go away over the weeks that followed. Eventually positive plans were laid with Charles' and Mary's blessing; Julian would borrow his family's camper van – not a new vehicle but roadworthy and watertight – and they would enjoy a holiday driving through Europe as well as re-uniting Marie with her Mother again, if only for a week or so.

Tereza's estimate to Maruška of 'early in the New Year' proved optimistic, but when Julian could be spared from the farm in the late Spring they set off.

It was at the Border post from Austria into Czechoslovakia that Julian had his first taste of Communist living. Not that they were held up: he just wasn't used to Customs Officers carrying guns. 'Not really civilised,' he thought, 'not like Dover.'

Nor were the roads kind to his camper van; it rattled and shook over gaps in the concrete slabs which passed for highways; there were bicycles in battalions to be avoided and large, heavy lorries belching diesel fumes which commandeered the centre of the roadway.

Some ten miles or so from the city of Prague, they entered the concrete forest. Large blocks of flats, two, three storeys high; row upon row of them; dirty, sickly white.

No life, no colour, no vitality.

As they neared the city boundary there began another hazard – trams. 'Which side do I overtake on?' Julian wondered, as his vehicle bumped and slithered on a tramline junction. "Don't think we have any trams in England," he murmured to Marie, "unless they still run in Blackpool."

But if he was disconcerted by the approach, he had to admit that the City itself was magic.

When they reached Bubeneč, Tereza, not given to displays of emotion, hugged her daughter, kissed her, held her at arm's length, hugged her again. Marie shed tears of joy and, arms linked, they started to climb up the four flights of stairs. "The lift," she said to Julian over her shoulder, "is not working again." When they reached Tereza's flat, Julian was astounded at its size. "Why," he said to Marie, "this is smaller than your flat at home. And you said that you had to share this with your Mother! No wonder she told you to stay in England ..."

They packed so much into that week. Julian, accepted immediately by Tereza, was shown all the sights and sounds of the medieval city; met so many of Marie's and Tereza's friends and relations; drank quantities of Czech beer at tables on the pavements outside bars; ate at Tereza's favourite restaurant in a cellar not far from Charles Bridge surrounded by more friends and relations, and developed leg muscles he never knew he had climbing and descending the stairs between the flat and street level.

One evening, Julian was introduced to a youngish woman who seemed a particular friend.

She was Maruška, and with Marie translating, asked him many questions about life in England. By the end of the evening, they were teasing Julian unmercifully.

"Maruška asks why my Mother's letters are addressed to 'U.K.' and not England?"

"Tell her that letters would still reach us if they were addressed to England."

"She wants to know if England and the U.K. are the same place."

"Yes. Well, no. You know, Marie. England is part of the U.K., the United bit includes Scotland, Wales and Northern Ireland. You can explain it to her."

Whatever it was that Marie said to Maruška, it was certainly Marie who, straight-faced, said that Maruška had seen 'G.B.' on the back of Julian's van, and she wanted to know what it meant and how it differed from U.K.

Julian realised that Maruška had not visited Tereza's flat that week and so could not have seen his vehicle parked outside. "Tell her," he said thoughtfully, "that when we say England, we could mean Great Britain, or we could mean the United Kingdom, or even at a pinch the British Isles, but we would never mean England!" Both Marie and Julian laughed happily at the 'Caught you!' riposte, while Tereza smiled indulgently, "Private English joke," she said, but Maruška looked wistfully at Marie and her Englishman.

Too soon it was time to leave. There were presents to buy for the family in England; Thank you's and Goodbyes to say, promises to return, luggage to load, and Goodbyes and hugs and kisses all over again. A final wave and out through the ring of concrete; through the countryside to the Border, and that Customs Post again where they joined a long queue of vehicles. It had been a two-hour drive, so they broke open the sandwiches and a flask of coffee while they waited. When they were only a few vehicles away from the buildings, a Customs man came down the side of the queue and asked for their Passports.

They had moved up a couple of places when the Customs man returned accompanied by two others, one a woman, and two soldiers – at least that was what Julian presumed they were. They had rifles cradled in their arms and took up positions at the front of the vehicle. One Customs man spoke across Julian to Marie who translated. "They want you to move over to that parking space on the right there."

The guards moved and indicated Julian to follow. They were now off the roadway, just short of the Customs post and some thirty yards from the barrier.

Again, Marie was spoken to in Czech. "Switch off the engine, they say."

The doors were opened; more instructions. "They are ordering us out. Julian, I don't like this."

Maruška gazing across the Vltava river in Prague.

This was the first time Julian had been confronted with orders given by a man with a gun and he reacted with surprising calmness. As he swung himself out he slipped the ignition keys into a trouser pocket, turned and shut the driver's door. He was about to lock it when he saw Marie being escorted towards the Customs building by the woman Officer, her hand firmly on Marie's elbow.

"Hey, you!" he shouted. "Marie!" and he started after them.

One of the soldiers immediately blocked his way, holding his rifle horizontally in front of Julian.

He heard Marie shout over her shoulder, "Don't provoke them!" while her escort shook Marie's elbow and urged her forward. Julian saw them disappear into the Customs building and the door shut. 'God!' he thought, 'What do I do now?'

The second soldier appeared, and indicated to Julian a low wall at the side of the hard-standing. The first made pushing movements and – though he could not understand a word of their instructions – it was clear that he had to retreat to this wall. This he did, very slowly, and there the soldiers motioned him to sit down.

One stayed with him; the other joined the Customs men at the van. They opened the rear door and took out a large canvas holdall. This was the last luggage loaded, and contained the 'Wanted on Voyage' stuff:– spare sweaters, night attire, toiletries, spare shoes ... One man brought it round to the side of the van and opened it. He did not bother to search through it – merely turned it upside down and tipped the entire contents onto the roadway. Then he riffed through by spreading everything out with his foot.

Julian was on his feet. "You can bloody well pick it all up again!" he shouted. Immediately that rifle was across his chest. The soldier, with a wide grin, spoke briefly and pointed at the wall. That he was enjoying the show so far, and anticipating what was to follow, was evident. Julian, remembering Marie's warning sat again, his face red with anger. The Customs man, acting as if he never heard Julian's outburst, had fetched a suitcase from the van. This received similar treatment.

Most of their personal belongings were now strewn on the ground. Drivers waiting to go through Customs watched the performance impassively, taking care not to appear too interested.

Julian saw one Customs official examine a small gift-wrapped box. He held it to his ear and shook it. Then he sniffed it. Finally, he ripped off the wrapping and opened the box.

It contained a lovely piece of Bohemian glass – a present for Mary. Losing interest, he dropped the box and the glass onto the roadway and dived back into the van. The soldier at Julian's elbow laughed with delight and banged the butt of his rifle on the ground.

Then they found, under the driver's seat, the tool box. This proved a great interest, the contents were tipped out and examined carefully; finally a few were put back. Julian ceased to watch: he sat, his head in his hands, totally impotent. Bad as this treatment of the vehicle was, he was more concerned about Marie. What had happened to her? Where was she? What were they doing to her?

But they hadn't finished with the van. Now they ripped out the door panels, carefully examining the spaces revealed. Underneath the rear of the van, they found the spare wheel. This was removed, and to ensure there was nothing hidden within, the air was released and the tyre stamped on vigorously. At last, they appeared satisfied, made notes on a clipboard and sauntered away leaving the second soldier guarding the van.

It was all of a further fifteen minutes before the door of the Customs building opened and Marie was escorted out. She was red-eyed and red-faced, dishevelled and distraught.

Julian ignored his guard, ran over and put his arm around Marie. There was no attempt to stop him: they just stood and watched. Marie sobbed, "They say we are free to go."

Together they simply picked up everything off the ground and threw it into the van. They left behind broken glass, handkerchiefs, lipsticks, a broken Thermos – the detritus of a broken journey. Finally, Julian swung into the driver's seat, fished out the ignition key and started up.

Then Marie shouted, "Passports! They've still got our passports!"

Julian cut the engine, got out and walked up to the grinning Customs official. "Passports." he demanded, and held out his hand. The fellow took out a packet of cigarettes and a lighter; lit a cigarette and blew the smoke in Julian's face. Then he turned and slowly walked to the building. Julian stood his ground.

Some minutes later he returned with the Passports in one hand, tapping them against his other hand as if considering whether to return them or not. Finally, he seemed to have made a positive decision but at the last moment before they reached Julian's hand, he dropped them.

It was Julian's turn. He motioned to the official to pick them up.

They stood facing each other with full eye contact, neither moving. Then as if feeling that the whole business had gone on long enough, the second Customs man moved over, picked the Passports up and pushed them into Julian's top pocket. They were waved through the stream of waiting traffic and through the barrier. They were in Austria.

As soon as he could, Julian pulled off the road and switched off. He moved over and took Marie in his arms, gently stroking her hair. She had been sobbing quietly, her hands pressed hard together. Thus they stayed for … Julian could not tell how long. It was now dark. The van was rocked by the heavy lorries as they passed on the same side.

Eventually, he whispered, "What did they do to you?"

It was some moments before Marie spoke.

"She took me into a small room. There was just a chair, but they would not let me sit down. There were no windows but one of the soldiers came in as well and leant against the door ... Then the woman told me to take my clothes off. I had to, Julian, they would have taken them off me if I had refused ... She said so ... So I did, slowly, just one at a time ..."

There was another pause before Marie continued.

"The woman examined each garment, starting with the label. She felt all round as if I might have something hidden in the lining. When I was down to my underclothes I stopped ... but she said to go on ... I asked the soldier to turn his back but he just leered. So I turned to face the wall away from him, and handed my bra and panties over my shoulder."

Marie paused. Julian felt sick with apprehension. He stroked and cuddled her.

"Want to go on?" he whispered. She shook her head. The lights of passing vehicles lit the wrecked inside of the van: they did not notice. The noise reverberated round the empty shell of the camper: they did not hear it.

Marie sobbed as if living every moment of her torture all over again. Julian held her tight. He thought back over the last ten hours of anger and anguish, and came to several decisions.

The first lights of dawn were visible when he finally laid her down along the bench seat; spread his jacket over her, and went to make some rough order out of the chaos in the back of the van. Then he drove on – looking for breakfast.

Julian had phoned ahead; they would be coming straight to Charles and Mary's place. Marie was very tired and would be staying the night there rather than going to her own flat.

They arrived mid-evening and after a brief supper, Marie went to her old room and fell asleep, exhausted. Then Julian told Charles and Mary exactly what had happened at the Border post.

"I don't know now whether I did right," he said. "All my instincts were for having a go; two of them I could have thrown over the hedge with one hand, but then ... would the others have fired those guns? I just didn't know, and Marie shouted that warning not to wind them up. Should I have pushed him away and followed Marie when that woman took her off?"

"No," Charles said firmly. "You did absolutely the right thing."

"But I must have appeared such a coward, especially to Marie being marched off on her own like that!"

"No," repeated Charles. "You can replace your clothes and things; you can always get another vehicle if that bothers you, but you couldn't replace Marie, and she couldn't replace you if they'd shot you there and then."

"Would they have done that?"

"Well, it might have provoked an international incident ... it would have been resisting arrest ... threatening a Customs Official, that sort of thing. All their witnesses, of course."

There was a brief silence.

"Do you know what they were looking for?" asked Mary. "Why pick on you – just two young people on a holiday? What did they think you were smuggling?"

"Yes, I asked Marie that. She thinks it was all a pretence to get back at her. They knew she was Czech – from her speech, presumably, so they regarded her as a sort of traitor and just wanted to humiliate her."

"Yes, that figures," Charles pondered. "Sort of thing they would do, and delight in doing."

"O, they enjoyed it alright," rejoined Julian. "But I'm sure of one thing; next time we're going to do it differently. I'm not risking Marie going through that again."

Then he turned to Mary. "By the way, you know that Traveller's Cheque you gave me – as a sort of insurance. Marie said she felt dirty in those clothes even after she'd had a bath at the hotel, so we went out, cashed the cheque and bought her a complete set of new ones. I'll pay you back – soon as I've been home."

"No, you won't," retorted Mary. "You did quite the right thing. Just stop blaming yourself. Now are you going to stay for a drink and something to eat?"

"No, thanks. I'd better be off and catch up with the farm news." He got up, stretched, and walked to the door.

There he paused, turned and said, "You know, if Marie will have me, I want to marry her. That alright with you?"

"That would be fine with us," replied a startled Charles.

"That's alright then." said Julian, and left the room.

And that in one sense is the end of the story, and in another just the beginning.

Marie and Julian did go back to Prague once more by road. Almost everything they took with them, clothing, footwear and so forth, they left at Tereza's flat. They departed Czechoslovakia by a different Border post – had the Customs Officials bothered to look, they would have found the English vehicle almost empty.

A year later, Marie and Julian flew to Prague with hand luggage only. All they needed for a week's stay was already there and that set the pattern for future visits. It is likely that three topics were discussed.

First, the possibility of Tereza visiting England. Permission was given for her to take a short holiday from which she duly returned to Prague. There was never any doubt about that; she remained devoted to her friends and to the city in which she was born. Permission thereafter seemed to be given as a matter of course so her English holidays became longer, until by the mid-Nineties she was spending up to six months of each year with Marie, but she always went back to her beloved City, and the flat in Bubeneč where she still had, occasionally, to climb four flights of stairs.

Secondly, Maruška's wish to visit England. It was arranged that she could go for a short holiday (her application made no mention of Marie) and after much thought, she decided not to return to Czechoslovakia. She is now – as this story is written – a teaching nurse at a large hospital in England.

Thirdly, a wedding. Julian and Marie were married in 1974; Julian took over the farm, and the newly-weds took over the farmhouse. There is no doubt that, at first, it was hard work; and in Marie's case acclimatising to a new role, new surroundings and fresh faces.

Her days followed Julian; her meal times were his. Her weeks and months were now dictated by the seasons; by agricultural necessities. She became familiar with farm animals and farm machinery, and learnt to share her husband's economic hopes and despairs. She learnt also to keep out of the way when deadlines for completion of Forms and Returns were imminent. Gradually, they made it a success; Marie acquired her own dog and then her own car. She grew in confidence, made friends within the farming fraternity, and became known in the local community.

In due course a son, Gerald, was born followed two years later by another son, Charles.

They were the summit of Tereza's visits: for her the pleasure of seeing her Grandsons growing up in freedom, not fear; in happiness, not despair. She spoke to Charles and Mary not about the past but the future for her family. There was no trace of regret for her own lost years, no self-pity but great joy for her daughter and her Grandsons.

Now Gerald and Charles have grown into young men; staunch supporters of the countryside; both capable fellows who seem destined to be – in time – custodians of their own acres.

Marie and Julian have celebrated thirty years of married life; both have contributed much to the local community, and Marie – though proud to have justified her second nationality – now has her own flat in the city of her birth.

In central and eastern Europe, the stranglehold of communism gradually waned. The era of Gorbachev and *glasnost* brought some relief to those who longed for liberty, an era that culminated in the late 80's and early 90's. There were anti-communist riots and strikes in Czechoslovakia in November 1989, just about the time when the Berlin Wall, that hated symbol of repression, was opened up to the divided citizens. Like a pack of dominoes on end, the fall of the Wall meant the fall of the East German Cabinet and Hans Modraw, a liberal reformer, became Prime Minister.

Back in Prague, Miloš Jakeš, the Communist Party Leader and the entire ruling politburo resigned. In the last week of November, crowds marched through the streets chanting the names of 'Dubček' and 'Václav Havel', a leading Opposition figure who had been imprisoned by the Communist Party as an agitator. (As early as 1983, the BBC's correspondent, John Simpson, had obtained an interview with Havel. He is quoted as saying, "The Police, the forces of the State, can do nothing to us because we are free men and women. Free inside our minds, I mean.") Dubček, emerging from twenty years in total obscurity, addressed the crowds who packed Wenceslas Square and declared,. "We have been too long in darkness. Once already we have been in the light, and we want it again ... "

In Prague it was a peaceful change, but not everywhere in Europe was it so handled. On Christmas Day 1989, Nicholai Ceausescu, dictator of Romania, and his wife, were both summarily executed by a firing squad. Old scores were settled but legacies lingered on. Romania is still in desperate need of international help.

On New Year's Eve, Václav Havel was installed as the new President of Czechoslovakia and his first promise was free elections. Alexander Dubček became the Chairman of the Federal Assembly but died in 1992 at the age of 71. He did not have long to enjoy his free country.

So much for the leaders, those whose policies dictated many of the events in this story.

What of Stanislav, with whom the story started? He is buried in a cemetery in Prague far from Kbely airfield from which he had taken off so many times. What really happened on that last flight will never be known: it is very likely that there was an official investigation into the accident, but the Report – if one was issued – remains unobtainable. Teresa was told that something went wrong with the aircraft and that remains the most likely cause. When the Communist Party took over in February 1948, the aircraft of British manufacture used by the Czechoslovak Air Force were deemed unsuitable and were replaced, gradually, by Russian-built aircraft. Until that process was complete, the Czechs used their Spitfires and Mosquitos, their Austers and Ansons. But no spares were ordered for engines or airframes.

When an aircraft went unserviceable, it was often withdrawn and parts used to keep other aircraft flying. But occasionally, major faults occurred in the air and rendered that aircraft uncontrollable. Sometimes the crew managed to bale out; sometimes there was such catastrophic failure that the crew suffered the same fate as their aircraft.The history of aviation contains many examples of brave men and women who survived the most unlikely escapades and ventures only to lose their lives in later accidents. To this category must Stanislav be allocated.

And what of the incidental figures? What became of Vladimír, that walking accident who spent years temporarily in charge of the Housing Department of the City authority? And his friend Novák, who worked for Janáček, the Head of the Supplies Section?

Vladimír's unit continued to grow mysteriously. Tereza virtually took control, training up the young women who were assigned to his department, while Janáček remained short of labour and ran Novák off his feet. It was a chance meeting with a very senior official outside working hours that finally let Janáček into the secret.

"Vladimír Roubíček? Well, I thought everyone knew! He's the son of the Commissar's sister and she's a real dragon by all accounts. When she wants something she just lays siege to the Commissar's home until he gives in. Young Vladimír only has to say to his mother that he's overworked and has no social life and there you are! Another young woman for the over-stretched Housing Department."

But as *glasnost* reached the City offices, Vladimír made a courageous decision. He resigned, and has since made a small fortune importing mobile phones. Of course, he employs Novák to do the leg-work for him …

VIII

Tereza

Tereza died in June 2000 while on holiday here in England. She had been ill for some time. At the Service of Thanksgiving for her life, Charles was asked to give the Address. This is what he said.

We are here to bid farewell to Tereza Židlická – wife to Stanislav; mother to Marie, Grandmother to Gerald and Charles, and friend to us all.

In her different relationships she was known by different names; her full name was shortened by her family to Terrie; she signed her letters to me, Tereza; many local people knew her simply as Mrs Z, but it was left to her Grandsons to encapsulate one of her outstanding qualities when they called her with affection, their 'little Chipmunk' – always busy, always working.

We remember her at the farm – as she would probably wish to be remembered – as a quiet figure in the background. A lady who preferred listening to talking (in what was for her, of course, a foreign language); a lady who preferred to be the force behind the Aga; the purveyor of delicious dumplings and gorgeous cakes; the doyenne of the dogs, and the scourge of wayward grandsons. While we all talked and laughed, she quietly removed the dishes and saw that all went smoothly for the guests.

And yet ... few of us here today have any conception of the life she had lead, nor I suspect would many of us have measured up to her strength of mental and physical courage, for she was a very brave lady. Fortune did not favour her. Born in Prague, she was only three when her father died of wounds while serving in the cavalry in Serbia in 1917. She was an only child.

Years later she was to show me the basement flat in which she grew up, and in which she sheltered from the German bombardment in 1939. We were spared the occupation of an invading army; she was not. She endured the fears; the rumours; the arrests, the executions – from which her own family was not spared.

In 1942, she met her future husband, Stanislav. After working for the underground, he re-joined the Czechoslovak Air Force in 1945 and the following year was posted to England with his Squadron. It was during this period that he and I met, and became good friends. Stanislav and Tereza were married back in Prague in December 1948, but by this time there was another occupation – that of the Communist regime. Again, Fortune did not favour her.; just less than four months later her new husband was killed in a flying accident. Marie was born posthumously the following September. Here was History repeating itself – this time Tereza bringing up her only child, by herself, in the most difficult circumstances.

THE MARIE STORY

Tereza at about the same age as Marie was when she came to England.

Of this time she told me ... you talked only in whispers; you kept your head down, watched everything carefully and never drew attention to yourself – whatever the circumstances. How many of us, I wonder, could do that, day after day; month after month; year after year? Some eighteen years later came, perhaps, one of the most difficult decisions that Tereza ever had to make. In August 1968, Russian troops marched into Prague. Marie was spending that summer holiday with us; that night she telephoned her Mother and asked if she might stay in this country. It was surely a measure of Tereza's love for her daughter that she was prepared for the inevitable separation in return for Marie's happiness.

The last message broadcast from Prague before the Russians stormed the transmitter was this, "Don't forget us! Remember us, even when our resistance has finished, and the rest of the world has found other things to think about." I like to believe Tereza's voice was in that message – for me, my family, for all of us. It was to be some four long years before she saw her daughter again.

Perhaps Fortune was smiling on her now, but in disguise. We all know the outcome – Marie's marriage to Julian; the arrival of her Grandsons, and the happy occasions that all five enjoyed both here in England, and on holidays abroad and back in Prague. I also believe that Tereza came to appreciate her life on an English farm, and the company of the farming community. With its crops and livestock; with its wide skies and scattered villages, it became a security she had not known in earlier life – a comfort and solace in her later years. The freedom of the countryside represented for her an attitude of tolerance which enabled her to move about and talk without fear or restraint to anyone. She respected people for who they were, not what they were; and this is reflected by the esteem and affection in which she was held by local folk.

Tereza was a lady of her time, of the turbulent twentieth century. She was courageous – even in the last few weeks of her life when she knew the truth and tried to conceal it from her family lest it distress them. Generous of spirit; hard-working; immensely loyal to her fellow Czechoslovaks and the city of her

Tereza on an English farm about a year before she died.

birth where, appropriately, her ashes will rest. A presence has left us and we shall mourn her; grieve and sympathise with her family, with Julian and Marie, with Gerald and Charles.

IX

Marie – The last word

Shortly before the last General Election in this country, Marie wrote a letter to the local newspaper. This is what they printed.

Editor.

I was quite astonished when taking my husband to the Hospital on Friday 18th May, by the large numbers of Police present during Mr Blair's visit there. Had the majority of the County's Police Force been drafted to protect him from us lesser mortals just in case we should dare to ask some realistic questions?

It actually reminded me of my childhood spent in communist Czechoslovakia with hundreds of police about to make us behave as we were dictated to whenever our leaders came into our communities to tell us how well they were doing. The one slip up by Mr Blair's spin doctors was the absence of well-organised people waving 'pro' Mr Blair banners and chanting his name frequently. It just lacked the organised supporters to make their mission as complete as it used to be in any communist state when the people had to greet their leaders.

Come on ... Wake up Great Britain people and hang onto your precious freedom before it slowly slips away.

Yours, etc.